FOOD POLITICS

WHAT EVERYONE NEEDS TO KNOW

D1362232

FOOD POLITICS
WHAT EVERYONE NEEDS TO KNOW

ROBERT PAARLBERG

Second Edition

OXFORD
UNIVERSITY PRESS

OXFORD
UNIVERSITY PRESS

Oxford University Press is a department of the University of Oxford.
It furthers the University's objective of excellence in research, scholarship,
and education by publishing worldwide.

Oxford   New York

Auckland   Cape Town   Dar es Salaam   Hong Kong   Karachi
Kuala Lumpur   Madrid   Melbourne   Mexico City   Nairobi
New Delhi   Shanghai   Taipei   Toronto

With offices in

Argentina   Austria   Brazil   Chile   Czech Republic   France   Greece
Guatemala   Hungary   Italy   Japan   Poland   Portugal   Singapore
South Korea   Switzerland   Thailand   Turkey   Ukraine   Vietnam

Oxford is a registered trademark of Oxford University Press in the UK and
certain other countries.

Published in the United States of America by
Oxford University Press
198 Madison Avenue, New York, NY 10016

© Oxford University Press 2013

All rights reserved. No part of this publication may be reproduced,
stored in a retrieval system, or transmitted, in any form or by any means,
without the prior permission in writing of Oxford University Press, or
as expressly permitted by law, by license, or under terms agreed with
the appropriate reproduction rights organization. Inquiries concerning
reproduction outside the scope of the above should be sent to the Rights
Department, Oxford University Press, at the address above.

You must not circulate this work in any other form
and you must impose this same condition on any acquirer.

Library of Congress Cataloging-in-Publication Data
Paarlberg, Robert L.
Food politics : what everyone needs to know / Robert Paarlberg.—Second
edition.
pages cm
Includes bibliographical references and index.
ISBN 978–0–19–932238–1 (pbk. : alk. paper)—ISBN 978–0–19–932239–8
(hardcover : alk. paper)
1. Agriculture and state.   2. Food supply.
3. Food—Marketing.   4. Nutrition policy.   I. Title.
HD1415.P12 2013
338.1'9—dc23
2013008726

1 3 5 7 9 8 6 4 2
Printed in the United States of America
on acid-free paper

CONTENTS

13 Food Safety and Genetically Engineered Foods   184

PREFACE TO THE SECOND EDITION OF
FOOD POLITICS

I am pleased that Oxford University Press is publishing this second edition of *Food Politics: What Everyone Needs to Know*. In the fast moving world of food politics, new initiatives and controversies are continuously emerging, so readers will stand to benefit from this updated version of the original 2010 book.

Those familiar with the first edition of *Food Politics* will notice a number of important additions and changes here. Prominent among these is a new chapter addressing the politics of meat consumption, livestock farming, and fisheries. In the first edition, issues surrounding meat and livestock were scattered throughout the book in a less organized fashion, and the first edition said nothing about fish, a dietary resource of rapidly growing importance. This second edition also provides more discussion of agriculture's link to both water and climate change. I offer more about agriculture and the environment in general, including the continuing evolution of agriculture in rich countries toward "precision" systems that help lessen environmental damage. These systems have emerged rapidly in the commercial production sector, yet precision farming remains underappreciated in political debates. In this second edition I have also added a short concluding chapter on the future of food politics.

It was interesting that the first edition of this book produced some heated food politics of its own. Academic reviewers offered praise for the book, but one predicted that it would "drive food activists half-nuts" because it challenged some of their deepest orthodoxies. In fulfillment of this prediction, one activist went so far as to organize a prolonged public campaign against the book. No significant factual errors had been found in the first edition, but my critics did find plenty of arguments and conclusions to disagree with. For those interested in my one public response to this campaign, a short letter I published in the *Chronicle of Higher Education* in April 2012 can be found online. Respectful engagement with critics is part of the duty of scholars, even when a final reconciliation of differences will remain impossible. My approach here is to present the facts, trying at the same time not to ignore or misrepresent the perspective of those who hold different beliefs or draw different conclusions.

Political perspectives are invariably shaped by personal experience. In the first edition of this book I explained that my father was raised on a farm in Indiana, passing along to me an agrarian heritage that I proudly retain. I also mentioned that my concern for rural poverty and undernutrition dates from an early visit I made to India and Nepal, where my brother was serving as a Peace Corps volunteer. I have returned to study and record the evolution of farming in Asia and Africa numerous times since. In this book I try to keep my own personal perspectives in their place, but I cannot pretend they are absent. I take pride in my independence; in my long career as a university-based academic, I have never been funded or employed by any private company. My research has sometimes been funded by private foundations, and sometimes by governmental or intergovernmental agencies, but most often I have turned for research support to the generosity of my home institution, Wellesley College. In my role as a policy expert, I have had occasion to meet with corporate executives, and a decade ago I did agree to participate, alongside other academics and NGO leaders, in a series of external "sounding board" meetings with scientists and executives from the Monsanto Company, a controversial actor on the food politics landscape, but I asked not to be paid. As for my political leanings, I have always been a registered Democrat. Yet my views on food and farming do not fall neatly into partisan categories. The sections of this book that address food markets and science-based farming are likely to irritate the political Left and please the political Right, but the sections that address food companies, development assistance, climate change, and animal welfare will do the opposite.

In modern societies where few people still work the land as full-time farmers, and where markets offer an ever wider range of choices about what to eat, how to eat, and how much to eat, the politics of food has come to extend far beyond material questions of who gets what, or even Left versus Right. Nor is there a unified academic perspective. Biologists and economists routinely disagree with philosophers, ecologists, and sociologists. Originally trained as a political scientist, I try to remain open to multiple perspectives.

I share with food activists considerable dissatisfaction with today's world of food and farming. Too much of our food is unhealthy, too much of our farming is still unsustainable, and too many of our rural societies remain unjust. Our world of more than 7 billion food consumers (heading toward 10 billion) is still not being adequately or properly fed. I may be less scolding toward the present than some, and less pessimistic about the future, but I concede the value of pessimism, for motivating political systems to act. I offer this updated and revised edition of *Food Politics: What Everyone Needs to Know* as a new starting point for problem solvers of every stripe, in hopes that it can motivate action as well.

FOOD POLITICS

WHAT EVERYONE NEEDS TO KNOW

1

AN OVERVIEW OF FOOD
POLITICS

What is food politics?

Since biblical times, the policies of governments have shaped food and farming. The book of Genesis (47:24) records that in Egypt the pharaoh took 20 percent of all food production from his farmers as a tax. Governments in Africa today often burden farmers with taxes nearly as large, usually imposed indirectly through price manipulations by state-monopoly marketing agencies, or through overvalued currencies that implicitly tax the producers of all tradable goods. Meanwhile, governments in wealthy industrial countries usually provide direct and indirect subsidies to farmers, typically at the expense of both taxpayers and consumers. Understanding the dynamics behind such differences in agricultural societies versus post-agricultural societies is one of the goals of this book.

The food and farming sectors of all states, ancient and modern, foster considerable political activity. Rural food producers and urban food consumers have divergent short-term interests, so they will naturally compete to use the far-reaching powers of the state (e.g., collecting taxes, providing subsidies, managing exchange rates, regulating markets) to pursue a self-serving advantage. We describe such struggles over how the risks and gains from state action are allocated within the food and farming sector as "food politics." The distinctive feature of food politics is not just social contestation about food, but political competition to shape the actions of government. If you and I have a personal disagreement over the wisdom of eating junk food, that is not food politics, but if you and your allies organize to advocate new government regulations on junk food (for example, restricting what can be served in public school cafeterias), the disagreement then becomes food politics.

Is food politics driven by material interests or by social values?

Food politics is driven by both. In poor countries where a preponderance of all citizens still work in the farming sector and where large numbers of citizens still find it difficult to afford enough food, material interests will tend to dominate. In these societies, food and farming are still a large part of material welfare for all. In wealthy post-agricultural societies, however, farmers have become few in number, and most consumers are easily able to afford an adequate diet. In these societies, material conflicts around food and farming will persist, but social values—such as values regarding the natural environment, or toward animal welfare, or toward the preservation of traditional culture—will begin to play a larger role.

Country by country, food politics is often similar to other kinds of politics. In democratic societies, it revolves around the actions of elected government officials who confront pressures from organized non-governmental groups in society. In authoritarian or one-party states, it emerges from official rulings issued by political elites who are less accountable to society. Yet food politics does exhibit a consistent pattern across all countries, linked to the larger process of industrial development. Industrialization brings rapid productivity growth to farming as well as manufacturing, but it also results in a rapid loss of farm jobs, as fewer people are needed to produce food. In the United States, the share of farmers in the work-force fell from 50 percent in 1870 to only 3 percent by 1990, and only 1 percent today. Meanwhile, urban population and income growth boosts the demand for food and brings a rapid expansion of food-processing companies, private food transport and distribution systems, supermarkets, and food service restaurants. At every step in this process, politically motivated groups of farmers and non-farmers, private companies, and non-governmental organizations struggle to shape government policy in a manner consistent with their preferences.

As the farming sector loses numerical strength, organized groups of farmers will begin to take some of the strongest political actions. In the United States, Europe, and Japan during the peak decades of industrialization in the mid-twentieth century, farmers organized to demand escalating subsidies from the state, and they prevailed. Farm lobbies were strong, and by the 1980s, farmers in Japan were getting $23 billion worth of farm program benefits from their government, farmers in the United States were getting $26 billion, and farmers in the European Community were getting $33 billion.

These wealthy societies have now moved into a post-industrial stage, and the subsidy policies originally set in place to benefit conventional farmers are being criticized by consumer advocates who want food to be nutritious as well as cheap, by environmentalists who oppose conventional farming methods, and also by a new generation of alternative farmers promoting production systems that are small-scale, diversified, local, and organic. In this setting, a new political dynamic emerges: "food movement" advocates push hard to bring their alternative preferences into the mainstream.

Political struggles over food and farm policy within these democratic societies are divisive and polarizing because the opposing positions incorporate conflicting social values, which always makes compromise difficult. Debates over conventional versus organic farming, or over industrial versus small-scale livestock production, or over supermarkets versus farmers' markets provide little space for policy agreement. Yet the policies that emerge in democratic states are typically more successful than those within authoritarian or one-party systems. In authoritarian states, where individuals and groups in society lack any institutionalized political voice, serious food policy errors are frequently made. In fact, serious famines have only taken place in non-democratic societies. The worst famine ever recorded took place in China in 1959–1961, during the so-called Great Leap Forward, when radical policy decisions made by the unchallenged ruler Mao Zedong caused an estimated 30 million people to die of hunger. The world's most recent famines have also taken place in non-democratic states: in North Korea after 1996, and in southern Somalia in 2011.

Is food politics a global or a local phenomenon?

According to one widely quoted legislative leader in the United States, Representative Tip O'Neill, "All politics is local." This holds true for much of food politics. Analysts like to talk about the "world food system," but to a large extent the world remains divided into many separate and highly diverse national or even local food systems.

Despite the growth of international food markets, roughly 90 percent of all food never enters international trade. It is still consumed within the same country where it was produced. In poor agricultural countries, a great deal of the food supply is still consumed within the same community that produced it, or even by the same individual who produced it. In South Asia today, international markets for agricultural commodities play only a small role in personal food outcomes. Only 6 percent of wheat consumption in South Asia is supplied through imports, and only 1 percent of rice consumption is imported. When understanding the food politics of such regions, it will be local weather, local markets, local social conditions, and the actions of local leaders that will matter most.

The heaviest users of world food markets are today's rich overfed countries, not poor underfed countries, and much of what the rich import is feed for animals, not food for direct human consumption. For example, the world's biggest corn importer by far is Japan, which uses this grain to produce beef, pork, poultry, milk, and eggs. Japan is willing to import corn for animal feed, but its government maintains tight restrictions on the import of rice, the traditional food staple. Governments in South Korea, India, China, and many poor countries use similar border control measures to avoid dependence on imports of staple foods. These policies frustrate food-exporting countries such as the United States, and they violate the pro-trade advice of international bodies such as the World Trade Organization (WTO), but international food markets have only as much room to operate as separate national governments will allow.

In addition to being highly compartmentalized, the world's food system is one in which nutrition outcomes diverge dramatically country by country, and also person by person within countries. When it comes to food and agriculture, the world is not flat. The wealthy regions of Europe, North America, and Northeast Asia are agriculturally productive and well fed (increasingly, they are overfed), while the less wealthy regions of South Asia and tropical Africa are still home to hundreds of millions of farmers who are not yet highly productive and large numbers of people who are not adequately nourished. In Sub-Saharan Africa today, about 60 percent of all citizens are farmers or herdsmen living in the countryside, and one out of three is chronically undernourished. In South Asia, roughly 400 million farmers earn less than $1 a day, and approximately 25 percent are undernourished. The needs of these people remain unmet in part because their national governments continue to underinvest in the rural roads, water, power, schools, and clinics needed to escape poverty. The rural poor have scant political power (many are women who cannot read or write), so they can be easy for governments to ignore.

In some institutional settings, the politics of food and farming is being addressed within a global frame of reference. For example, agricultural trade restrictions are the subject of periodic global negotiations at the WTO, and global food assistance needs are addressed by the United Nations World Food Programme (WFP). Yet national and local food and farming systems remain significantly separate and divided, thanks to geographic distance, weak transport infrastructures, divergent cultural and dietary traditions, and large gaps in purchasing power. These diverse and largely separate food systems are shaped by the policies of separate national governments, many of which have different characteristics and divergent priorities. As a result, most policy success or failure in food and farming takes place nationally or locally, rather than globally. Thinking globally is good advice when working on problems such as climate change, telecommunications policy, or international finance, but when considering the politics of food and agriculture, it is often more useful to think nationally, or even locally.

Who are the most important actors in food politics?

In every setting where food politics takes place, organizations with divergent preferences will compete for influence. Organizations representing consumers will usually want food prices to be low, while advocates for farmers usually want high prices (except livestock producers, who will want cheap grain to feed to animals). In addition, farmers' organizations will typically join shoulder to shoulder to resist tight environmental regulations in their sector, and will be supported by the powerful industries that supply them with inputs such as fertilizer and pesticides. Groups claiming to speak for consumers will line up against food and beverage companies when the issue is taxes on junk food or nutrition labeling requirements.

In countries with democratic political systems, each of these groups will cultivate its own special friends and supporters inside government, especially within elected legislatures. In the United States, the organizations seeking benefits for commercial farmers are known as "farm lobbies," and they make generous campaign contributions to members of the agricultural committees of Congress, ensuring that once every five years those members will propose new legislation (a new "farm bill") renewing the costly entitlement programs that provide income subsidies to farmers. To guarantee a majority vote for the bill, provisions will be added to win support from potential critics such as urban consumers, humanitarian organizations, and environmentalists, in a standard legislative tactic known as a "committee-based logroll." Taxpayers will usually be the biggest losers when the logs start to roll.

Has the politics of food and agriculture recently been changing?

In today's advanced industrial and post-industrial societies, especially in Europe and North America, the politics of food and agriculture is undergoing significant change. There was a time when food consumers in these societies wanted just four things: foods that were safe, plentiful in variety, more convenient to purchase and prepare, and lower in cost. Now consumers in these countries are beginning to demand other things as well, such as foods with greater freshness and nutritional value, foods grown with fewer synthetic chemicals, foods grown with a smaller carbon footprint, foods that are locally grown, and foods produced without harm to farm animals. Emerging tastes of this kind among increasingly affluent and aware consumers have not driven low-cost convenience foods off the market by any means, but niche markets are now growing rapidly for foods that are local, organic, "sustainable," or "humanely produced." These alternatives have recently risen to dominate social debates, and in the United States, advocates for these alternative approaches are now calling for a new social movement—a "food movement"—capable of exercising hard political power, not just soft cultural influence. In 2013, *New York Times* food columnist Mark Bittman likened the emergence of such a movement to several other historic struggles for change, such as the battle to abolish slavery and the long struggle to extend voting rights to women.

Within the political arena, however, lobbyists working on behalf of conventional food industries and large commercial farmers continue to retain the upper hand. Much to the frustration of food and nutrition activists, food writers, advocates for farm animal welfare, and proponents of organic or local farms, the food and farming sector continues moving toward greater consolidation, greater automation, more industrialization, and more rather than less globalization. But in cultural terms, the battle lines have been drawn, and the conventional food and farming industry knows that it is under attack. Political leaders, caught in the middle, find it impossible to satisfy both camps.

These new political battles over food and farming are also being projected outward, beyond today's post-industrial societies into middle-income transitional countries and even into poor countries that are still mostly agrarian in character. Through trade and foreign assistance policies, through foreign investment actions by multinational food companies, supermarkets, and restaurant chains, and also through the countervailing advocacy of non-governmental organizations opposed to conventional food and agriculture, rich post-industrial societies are exporting their new debates over food and farming to the rest of the world. In commercial terms, the food systems of the world remain imperfectly integrated; the terms of our food politics discussions and debates, however, have been globalized at a surprising pace.

2

FOOD PRODUCTION AND POPULATION GROWTH

Who was Thomas Malthus, and why did he see hunger as inevitable?

Thomas Robert Malthus was an English economist who authored in 1798 a highly influential treatise, *An Essay on the Principle of Population.* In this essay, Malthus argued that food production could never stay ahead of population growth because it would be constrained by farm land assets that can expand only slowly, while human population tends to grow exponentially. Malthus concluded, "The power of population is so superior to the power of the earth to produce subsistence for man, that premature death must in some shape or other visit the human race." By this, Malthus meant premature death from war, plague, illness, or widespread famine.

It was nothing new in 1798 to predict the occurrence of war, plague, and famine, as these had been recurring tragedies throughout human history. Yet it was entirely new to predict—as Malthus did—that these tragedies were sure to worsen in the future due to the inability of agriculture to keep pace with human fertility.

Was Malthus right? In 1798, when he wrote his treatise, the earth had a population only one-sixth as large as today, so the number of people has increased exponentially, just as Malthus foresaw. The frequency of premature death from hunger and famine has not increased, however. The much larger numbers of people living today tend to live longer and to be far better fed than they were in Malthus's time. In England, where Malthus wrote, life expectancy at birth doubled over the past 200 years, from 40 years to more than 80 years. Up to the present, then, Malthus has been spectacularly wrong.

Yet what about the next 200 years? The earth's population is still increasing, and determined Malthusians insist that his prediction may yet come true. Dramatic food production gains over the past two centuries allowed the human population to grow from 1 billion up to 7 billion without any increased frequency of premature death, but these gains may not be environmentally sustainable. If the earth's population increases to 10 billion, as is probable by 2100, a Malthusian limit of some kind may finally be reached.

Most suspect not. One study done at Rockefeller University in 2012 concluded that agricultural innovations worldwide had already halted the global expansion of agricultural cropland, even though both population and food consumption per capita were continuing to rise. This study projected that over the coming 50 years, 146 million hectares of land would actually be released from farming globally, an area two and a half times the size of France. If so, this would mark a decisive end to the cropland constraint that most worried Malthus.

Was Malthus ever influential?

Malthus was clearly wrong for the first two centuries after he made his prediction, but this did not prevent him from being highly influential, particularly among political elites in England in the nineteenth century. This led to damaging consequences, particularly in England's colonial territories. Thomas Malthus himself was at one point employed as a professor at the British East India Company training college, and his fatalistic views regarding hunger came to influence England's official policies under the Raj, enabling an indifferent attitude toward the "inevitable" famines that ravaged India during colonial rule. Malthusian thinking also worsened the horrible tragedy of the 1845–1849 Irish famine, when a potato blight decimated Ireland's principal food crop. England controlled Ireland at the time, and political elites in London did little to provide relief, in part because they judged the famine to be an inevitable Malthusian consequence of Irish parents producing too many children. In this case it was only because England's political elites embraced Malthusian fatalism that the tragic prediction came true.

Fortunately, the Malthusian prediction was failing elsewhere at this time because the assumption that food production would remain tightly constrained by the limited land area on earth had proved badly flawed. The land constraint was progressively lifted beginning in the nineteenth century, thanks to the application of modern science to farming. A cascade of new farming technologies emerged over the two centuries after Malthus wrote his *Essay*—especially synthetic nitrogen fertilizer and improved seed varieties—allowing crop production on existing farmland to skyrocket. An acre of land today can produce 10 times as much food as it could when Malthus wrote in 1798.

These science-based crop-yield gains were particularly dramatic during the second half of the twentieth century. In the United States, average corn yields increased from 34 bushels an acre in the 1940s to 121 bushels per acre by the 1990s and then to 147 bushels per acre by 2011. Yields of corn greater than 200 bushels an acre are now common among farmers using the best new seeds and the most sophisticated practices. Farm productivity increased so rapidly in the twentieth century that the price of food declined (the "real" price, discounting for inflation), even though population and food demand were both steeply on the rise. The real price of farm commodities paid by consumers fell by more than 50 percent in the United States between 1900 and 2000, despite unprecedented consumption increases driven by high income growth as well as population growth.

Malthus also misjudged long-term trends in human fertility. He assumed that birthrates would remain continuously high, thus failing to anticipate the reduction in family size that takes place when societies become wealthier and more urbanized. In urban society, the value of having large families for unskilled farm labor declines, and the payoff from concentrating education investments in fewer children increases. Fertility also tends to fall when more children begin surviving infancy thanks to improved medical practices, and once education and employment opportunities are extended to young women as well as young men. This always leads to later marriage and hence to fewer years of active childbearing per woman. Because of all these factors in combination, fertility drops sharply in all modern industrial societies, and population growth slows as a consequence.

In some European countries today, population is actually shrinking—and without any premature deaths from war, plague, or famine. In Estonia, the birthrate has recently declined from 2.1 children per woman (the rate of births necessary to keep the population at a constant number) to only 1.2 children per woman. Rapidly declining fertility is now notable as well in India, Indonesia, Brazil, and Mexico. These declines in fertility have reduced the United Nations (UN) projection of the earth's peak population from 12 billion down to just 10 billion. Malthus has thus been doubly wrong so far. He expected that fertility would remain high, in the face of lagging food production, but instead we see fertility dropping sharply, even as food production continues a rapid increase.

Are Malthusians still influential?

The last interlude of acute Malthusian anxiety came in the 1960s and 1970s, at a time of high population growth in Asia, particularly in India and Bangladesh. In 1967, William and

Paul Paddock, an agronomist and a former Department of State official, wrote a best seller titled *Famine 1975!* in which they projected that India would never be able to feed its growing population. The Paddocks even warned that it would be a mistake to give food aid to India because that would keep people alive just long enough to have still more children, leading to even more starvation in the future. Fortunately, this advice was not taken. The U.S. government delivered unprecedented quantities of food aid to India in the 1960s to offset poor harvests, and the larger donor community provided assistance for a significant upgrade in India's own long-term farming potential—an upgrade that came to be known as the "green revolution." Improved seeds and fertilizers allowed India's farmers to boost their production of wheat and rice dramatically, and by 1975, India was able to halt food aid deliveries completely without a famine.

Paul R. Ehrlich, an American entomologist who originally specialized in butterflies, made a parallel Malthusian argument in a 1968 best seller titled *The Population Bomb*. Ehrlich predicted that hundreds of millions would die in the 1970s due to excessive population growth. He even projected that by 1980 residents in the United States would have a life expectancy of only 42 years. Surprisingly, the book continues to be cited, illustrating the persistence of some Malthusian thinking despite actual experience.

Can we feed a growing population without doing irreversible damage to the environment?

Modern-day Malthusians often add both a dietary and an environmental component to their argument. Regarding diet, they note that each individual today is more likely to consume more animal products, compounding agricultural demands by requiring the production of more animal feed. Regarding environmental issues, they fear that pushing food production to keep pace with population will result in too many dry lands or forest lands cleared for farming, and too much groundwater or surface water used for farm irrigation. Biodiversity will be lost. Food production may increase in the short run, but eventually a combination of falling water tables caused by over-pumping, plus desertification caused by the plowing and grazing of dry lands, will push production gains into reverse. This will cause an even more extreme Malthusian collapse, because by then the human population will be even larger. Under this scenario, the most frightening thought is that we may have already exceeded the earth's capacity for *sustainable* food production without realizing it.

Eco-Malthusian "overshoot and collapse" projections of this kind have been in circulation at least since a 1972 report from an organization called the Club of Rome, titled *Limits to Growth*. Jared Diamond's 2005 best-selling book titled *Collapse: How Societies Choose to Fail or Succeed* also popularized the overshoot idea. Diamond's account of the disastrous fate of early peoples on Easter Island, Greenland, and the Maya in Central America was intended to drive home the importance of staying within eco-Malthusian limits. The weakness in Diamond's approach was that he could document vulnerabilities to overshoot and collapse only among pre-scientific societies, those lacking the innovation and adjustment potential found in today's advanced societies.

Is Africa facing an eco-Malthusian food crisis today?

While eco-Malthusian visions are not yet convincing for the world at large, they occasionally emerge as a popular way to understand the particular plight of Sub-Saharan Africa. In this region, efforts to expand arable land area to boost food production, so as to keep pace with population growth, have led to serious environmental damage in the form of forest loss and habitat destruction. Damage to cropland productivity has been severe as well, because population pressures on the land have led to reduced fallow times, hence a more rapid depletion of soil nutrients. This in turn has constrained food production. In some African countries, average yields per hectare for some crops have actually declined, and for Sub-Saharan Africa as a whole over the past several decades, total food production per person has barely increased. Between 1990 and 2010, the proportion of Africans undernourished fell slightly but remained close to 30 percent; due to population growth, this number increased to exceed 200 million.

Africa's food problems are severe, yet they do not take the form of a classic Malthusian trap, in which population growth outstrips food production potential. This is because food production in Africa today is far below the known potential for the region. African farmers today use almost no fertilizer (only one-tenth as much as farmers in Europe use), and only 4 percent of their cropland has been irrigated. Also, most of the cropped area in Africa is not yet sown with seeds improved through scientific plant breeding. As a consequence, average cereal crop yields per hectare in Africa are only about one-fifth as high as in the developed world. Africa is failing to keep up with population growth not because it has exhausted its potential but instead because too little has been invested in developing that potential. Typically in Africa today, governments spend only about 5 percent of their budget on any kind of agricultural investments, even though 60 percent of their citizens depend on the farming sector for income and employment. If food production fails to keep up because nobody invests to make farms more productive, that is certainly an acute public policy crisis, but it is not a classic Malthusian crisis.

Do Malthusians try to reduce population growth?

Thomas Malthus, in his day, never put much stock in efforts to control fertility. By the twentieth century, however, public and private interventions to encourage "family planning" were commonplace in the industrial world, where births per woman were rapidly declining anyway. It naturally became popular among modern-day Malthusians to advocate policy interventions to bring down fertility in developing countries as well. In 1974, at a United Nations World Population Conference in Bucharest, rich country governments told poor countries that they should slow population growth. Poor countries responded that what they really needed was more rapid economic growth.

International advocacy for aggressive family planning programs in the developing world fell out of favor later in the 1970s, when China's coercive one-child family policy led to female infants being killed by parents who wanted their one child to be a son, and when a state-sponsored sterilization policy in India led to explosive social tensions between Hindus and Muslims. In the decade between the 1974 World Population Conference in Bucharest and the 1984 International Conference on Population in Mexico City, fashion in the international assistance community shifted from rigid "supply-side" efforts to bring down fertility (e.g., giving men and women access to modern contraception) to a new "demand-side" approach that focused on reducing the desire for more children. This demand-side approach was advanced through an emphasis on income growth, increased child survival, and a promotion of education and employment opportunities for girls and young women.

Aggressive supply-side efforts to limit fertility also came under attack from the Christian Right in America in the 1980s as one part of a backlash against the 1973 Roe v. Wade Supreme Court decision that decriminalized abortion. Abortion opponents did not have the means to dictate policy inside the United States, but they did manage, beginning under the presidency of Ronald Reagan, to place tighter restrictions on foreign assistance programs that support family planning. Mindful that aggressive supply-side efforts at fertility control were no longer acceptable either to the political Left or the political Right, classic Malthusians retreated to the fatalistic pessimism of their original namesake.

Do Malthusians argue that we should reduce food consumption?

For Malthusians who no longer wish to advocate fertility control, the alternative is a call for reduced food consumption per capita. This argument was first popularized in 1971, by a food activist named Frances Moore Lappé, who wrote a widely influential book (3 million copies sold) titled *Diet for a Small Planet*. The book argued that meat consumption in rich countries was using up scarce land resources to grow grain to feed chickens, pigs, and cattle, when the grain should instead be used to prevent starvation in poor countries. Lappé argued against beef consumption in particular, observing that the protein that beef cattle consumed in feed was 21 times greater than the amount that they finally made available in their meat for human consumption. In a world of tightening food supply, perhaps the only escape would be a move toward vegetarian diets.

Reducing meat consumption in rich countries would be good for both human health and the environment in those rich countries, but it would have only a limited impact on food circumstances in poor countries. The International Food Policy Research Institute has used a computer model of global agricultural markets to estimate how much reduction in world hunger would result from a 50 percent cut in per-capita meat consumption from the current level in all high-income countries. Even under this extreme and unlikely scenario, the reduction in child hunger in poor countries would only be one-half of 1 percent. The reason is that meat consumption in rich countries is mostly a result of agricultural resource use in those same rich countries, not in places like Africa or South Asia where most hungry people reside. If rich countries ate less meat, the biggest market change would be an immediate reduction in total crop production in those same rich countries, not an increase in food production or consumption in poor countries. In much of Africa, meanwhile, becoming a vegetarian is not an option. On many dry lands in Africa, there is not enough rainfall to grow cereal crops, so the only source of food can be grass-fed animals, such as goats and cattle.

3

THE POLITICS OF HIGH FOOD PRICES

When did high food prices become a political issue?

Most recently high food prices became an intense political issue in 2007–2008, when international market prices for rice, wheat, and corn all spiked sharply upward at the same time. By April 2008, the price of maize (corn) available for export had doubled compared to 2 years earlier; rice prices had tripled in just 3 months; and wheat reached its highest price in 28 years. Riots broke out in a number of developing countries, and it seemed that hunger was certain to increase as well. The *New York Times*, in a lead editorial, declared these surprising changes a "world food crisis." Robert Zoellick, president of the World Bank, warned that high food prices were particularly dangerous for the poor, who must spend half to three-quarters of their income on food. "There is no margin for survival," he said.

A global financial crisis in 2009 soon caused international food prices to fall, but then in 2010 wheat prices increased sharply once more. Just as this second food price spike seemed to be passing by early 2012, a severe summer drought in the United States sent international corn prices spiking upward yet again.

This unusual series of international food price spikes between 2007 and 2012 reset global expectations and debates on food. The spikes were not just disruptive on their own terms; they called into question what had been a comforting assumption among most economists that over the long term agricultural commodity prices would fall rather than rise, thanks to continued farm productivity gains.

What caused these spikes in international food prices?

The cause of these international price spikes remains disputed to the present day. In retrospect, the most powerful explanation was a simultaneous change in the trade policies of countries exporting food into the international market. When food prices started to rise on domestic markets after 2006, numerous states began to restrict exports, to keep domestic prices low. When multiple states do this at the same time, domestic prices will be stabilized but less food will be available for export, so international prices spike upward.

More fundamental factors also played a role. Some economists stress a more fundamental supply-and-demand shift within the food sector, as low reserve stocks around the world were combining with high consumption growth in the newly wealthy states of Asia. Others said that the price shift came from beyond the food sector, specifically from higher fuel costs (the price of petroleum was also spiking in 2008), which drove up farm fertilizer costs and led to an increase in biofuel production, such as ethanol from corn, which diverted crops away from food markets.

Still others said that the spike came from speculative behavior on the part of international investors, who were moving their money into commodity markets (pushing up not just food and fuel prices but metals prices as well) because investment bubbles in stock markets and real estate were starting to deflate. In 2000 President Clinton had signed a Commodity Futures Modernization Act that reduced regulations governing the buying and selling of commodity futures by banks and securities firms. This opened the way for much more speculative buying and selling of food commodities, and the volume of these trades did increase sharply after 2006, with impacts on the spot market price. The futures contracts purchased by investors expire quickly, however, and only 2 percent of futures trades result in an actual delivery of goods, so most economists view speculative behavior in futures markets as an unlikely foundation for long-term international price trends.

One factor that could not be blamed was a slowdown in food production or in the growth of agricultural productivity. According to calculations from the U.S. Department of Agriculture, the annual rate of growth of total factor productivity in agriculture, in both North America and Asia, was significantly higher in the 15 years up to 2007 than it had been in the two decades prior to that period. Physical food shortages were not the cause of the 2008 price spike. Rice prices tripled on the world market in 2008, but global rice production had actually grown more rapidly than consumption during the previous year, leading to an increase in surplus stocks. Another explanation that could be dismissed was Chinese imports. Rapid income growth was driving up China's demand for food, but China's own production was also increasing, and China was actually a net exporter of rice, wheat, and corn when international prices were spiking in 2007–2008.

From inside the food and farming sector, the single biggest driver behind the exaggerated price spikes of 2007–2008 and 2010–2011 were export restraints, or fears of such restraints. In 2007 economic growth in Asia had been high, fuel prices were up, and inflation fears were on the rise. At this point, a number of countries decided to place restrictions on food exports, to protect their consumers from price inflation at home. China imposed export taxes on grains and grain products. Argentina raised export taxes on wheat, corn, and soybeans. Russia raised export taxes on wheat. Malaysia and Indonesia imposed export taxes on palm oil. Egypt, Cambodia, Vietnam, and Indonesia eventually banned exports of rice. India, the world's third-largest rice exporter, banned exports of rice other than basmati. When these export bans were instituted, international prices began spiking upward, which led importers to panic and to begin buying as much as they could before the price went higher. This of course worsened the price spike. Media reports of shortages proliferated, and panic buying even spread to the United States, where frightened consumers descended on stores to buy rice. In April 2008, the Costco Wholesale Corporation and Wal-Mart's Sam's Club had to limit sales of rice to four bags per customer per visit.

Memories of the 2008 export bans were still fresh in 2010, when a severe summer drought damaged grain production in Russia. Fearing a possible Russian export ban, importers accelerated their normal wheat purchases, which pushed the international price upward. This in turn pushed bread prices inside Russia to unacceptable levels. In midsummer the government did announce a temporary ban on all grain exports, which kept international prices high for at least the next 9 months.

The price spike of 2012 was less severe and was driven not by export bans but instead by an actual production shortfall, namely a severe drought that reduced total corn production in the United States by 13 percent. Episodic shortfalls of this kind are not without precedent. An earlier Midwest drought in 1988 had reduced U.S. corn production by 31 percent.

How many people became hungry when prices spiked in 2007–2008?

On this important issue experts also disagree. While the crisis was under way, the World Bank produced a hasty estimate, based on a computer model, which said that the higher international food prices were pushing an added 100 million people around the world into poverty. The media carelessly reported this as documenting 100 million more people going hungry. In the following year, however, the United Nations Food and Agriculture Organization (FAO) produced a calculation specifically asserting that the number of undernourished people worldwide had been pushed from 873 million in 2004–2006 up to 1.02 billion in 2009.

There were reasons from the start to be skeptical about the World Bank calculation. It was based on an artificial assumption that when international prices go up, national governments do not change their trade policies to offset the domestic impacts. In fact, it was trade policy changes of exactly this kind that had produced the exaggerated international price spike. The FAO calculation was harder at the time to second-guess, because it was not done in a transparent fashion. The consensus view in the media and in policy circles was that many more people had been made hungry, so the 1 billion number went essentially unchallenged.

Several years later, after the panic had passed, the FAO decided to reexamine its estimates, and in 2012 it published a remarkable revision. It adjusted its estimate for 2004–2006 upward, from 873 million to 898 million, and its estimate for 2007–2009 downward. It asserted that the numbers of undernourished people in the world had actually fallen in 2007–2009, during the first peak of the crisis, down to 867 million, and had remained near that lower level in 2010–2012, despite continued high prices and despite continued global population growth. These estimates implied that before, during, and after the peak of the crisis, the percentage of the world's population that was undernourished had actually fallen, from 14 percent down to 13 percent, and finally down to just 12 percent in 2010–2012.

Astute critics took these strangely revised FAO estimates as further evidence that all such calculations are unreliable. Still, the net increase in global hunger earlier estimated had almost certainly been an exaggeration. Most of the world's poorest people, those most vulnerable to hunger, were not well connected to international food markets, so price movements on the international market were not an especially powerful driver of human hunger. In rural Africa, for example, nearly all food remains local or homegrown, and much consists of products seldom traded on the international market, such as goat meat, cassava, yams, and millet. Rural road systems in these countries are so poor and transport costs so high that international price transmission into the countryside is weak. In South Asia, where most of the world's hungry people actually live, national governments have long used import restrictions to protect their domestic food markets from international price fluctuations. In 2011, for this reason, when the price of wheat was soaring on the world market, prices in India, on the streets of New Delhi, were actually falling.

Spikes in international food prices do create serious economic hardship for urban consumers in countries that have allowed themselves to become significantly dependent on food imports, including many in the Caribbean, Central America, and West Africa. The total number of people in this category may not be large, but as urban dwellers they have a large voice for expressing displeasure. For them, a sudden need to spend more for food will mean having less to spend on clothing, shelter, schooling, and other services. If the price increase is temporary, it may not produce much in the way of actual undernutrition, but it will immediately generate social and political unrest. Even if it does not lead to hunger, it will be certain to lead to anger, and urban anger is typically more dangerous to governments than rural hunger.

Do international food price spikes cause violent conflict?

The international food price spikes of 2007–2008 and 2010–2011 were credited with triggering a wide pattern of domestic social and political unrest. The 2007–2008 price event coincided with street protests or riots in Burkina Faso, Cameroon, Senegal, Mauritania, Côte d'Ivoire, Egypt, Morocco, Haiti, Mexico, Bolivia, Yemen, Uzbekistan, Bangladesh, Pakistan, Sri Lanka, and South Africa. In Haiti, food riots caused the death of five people and led to dismissal of the prime minister. Five protesters were also killed in Somalia. In Cameroon, at least 24 people were killed in the worst unrest in 15 years. In Pakistan, the army was deployed to stop the theft of food from fields and warehouses. When international wheat prices then re-spiked in the winter of 2010–2011, street demonstrations began in North Africa, where wheat flour, used for bread, is a basic staple. During the course of this "Arab Spring," governments were toppled in Tunisia, Libya, and Egypt.

Some analysts concluded, from these events, that international food price spikes had become a dominant new cause of social unrest and violent conflict around the world. When the third price spike began in 2012, this time driven by a U.S. drought, one respected academic warned, in a news interview, "We are on the verge of another crisis, the third in five years, and likely to be the worst yet, capable of causing new food riots and turmoil on a par with the Arab Spring." This dire prediction, so far, has not come to pass.

The Arab Spring, in particular, was a political upheaval that emerged from far more than just food prices. In Tunisia, where the protests began in December 2010, the people taking to the streets were not demanding cheaper bread. Instead they were calling for dignity, the removal of a corrupt government, and more jobs. The crisis began when a young man took his own life to protest not high food prices but an insult from an arro-gant government official. When the protests in Tunisia brought the government down, equally restless urban dwellers seeking political change in Libya and Egypt saw their opportunity and took to the streets for the same purpose. These urban dwellers in North Africa were not "hungry." In Cairo, the price of bread had been held low by government subsidies for so long that average daily calorie intake was at European levels, and dis-eases linked to obesity were a growing problem.

Have higher food prices triggered "land grabs" in Africa?

As would be expected, higher international food prices begin-ning in 2007 triggered larger investments in agricultural production worldwide, including the purchase or rental of underutilized farmland. Many investors—including private firms and sovereign wealth funds from China, India, South Korea, and oil-rich states in the Persian Gulf—saw land in Africa as potentially useful for the production of both food and biofuels. Because most agricultural land in Africa is legally under the control of governments rather than individual farmers (only about 10 percent of land in Africa is formally tenured), foreign investors began approaching African governments, including less scrupulous local officials, with offers to lease substantial areas of farming land. Between October 2008 and August 2009 alone, over 46 million hectares of farmland acquisitions were announced.

The obvious risk with such land deals is that the local farming or herding populations currently on the land will be uncompensated for any resulting disruption or destruction of their livelihood. If their land is taken over by investors for mechanized crop farming, or for plantation-style biofuels production, they run the risk of being displaced. Social justice non-governmental organizations (NGOs) were quick to brand this new wave of investments as a "land grab" and to demand stronger protection for local communities. The land grab terminology was apt, but in most cases it was not foreigners grabbing land directly from African farmers; it was African governments and government officials grabbing the land from their own citizens, then making a profit by selling or leasing it to foreigners. Africans saw what was going on and some protested. In Madagascar in 2009, violent street demonstrations broke out over a government plan to lease 1.3 million hectares of land to a South Korean corporation, Daewoo, to produce corn and palm oil. The government was replaced, and the plan was dropped.

When the United Nations Food and Agriculture Organization (FAO) studied these issues in 2012, it observed that despite many wild claims about land grabs in Africa, there were very little reliable data. Second, it saw that in many cases domestic investors had acquired more land than foreigners. Third, the implications for local farmers were seen to depend largely on the crop production systems selected by the investor. If an investor brings in new technology and infrastructure and makes contracted purchases from local farmers, there may be benefits for the rural poor.

The post-2007 burst in international land acquisition is still of uncertain significance. Many of the leases negotiated have been slow to result in actual investments on the ground. If international commodity prices fall back down to historical trend levels in the years ahead, the foreign investors might quickly back away. During an earlier price spike interlude in the 1970s, there was a similar burst of interest in acquiring African farmland to supply food to the wealthy Arab states of the Persian Gulf, and most of these investments evaporated after international prices declined in the decade that followed.

Have subsidies and mandates for biofuels contributed to higher international food prices?

Higher international petroleum prices were an important food price driver in 2007–2008, since they encouraged a diversion of crops such as sugar, corn, and soybeans away from food and feed markets to produce biofuels, such as ethanol from sugarcane and corn, or biodiesel fuel from vegetable oil. These market-driven diversions were then reinforced by government policies designed to subsidize or even require the use of food to produce still more fuel.

In December 2007 the U.S. Congress enacted an enlarged mandate for corn-based ethanol production, up from a prevailing 5 billion gallon level to a minimum of at least 15 billion gallons by 2015. Four years earlier, the European Union (EU) issued its own directive setting a target of 5.75 percent for "renewable" energy use in the transport sector by 2010. China had also been building state-owned ethanol plants, and in 2007 it emerged as the third-largest ethanol producer in the world, after the United States and Brazil. With policies such as these in place, 70 percent of all increased corn production globally between 2004 and 2007 went to biofuel use. Higher international corn prices were one result.

On the other hand, much of this diversion of food to fuel would have taken place without government encouragement, simply because of higher petroleum prices in the market. If the price of fossil fuel goes high enough, investors will start putting money into biofuels even without government subsidies or mandates. In the summer of 2008, when the price of petroleum topped $140 a barrel, much more U.S. corn was certain to be diverted to fuel use with or without a Renewable Fuel Standard. In fact, ethanol production capacity in the United States was expanded by private investments to a level significantly higher than the mandated capacity because oil prices were temporarily so high.

However, as an impression spread that biofuels policies were a contributor to high international food prices, political support for biofuels diminished around the world. As early as April 2008, at the early peak of the international food price spike, UN Secretary-General Ban Ki-moon called for a comprehensive review of biofuels policies. The UN's own special rapporteur on the right to food, Jean Ziegler, even branded biofuels "a crime against humanity" and called for a five-year moratorium. In 2011, a dozen international institutions issued a joint report calling for an end to distortive biofuel policies, especially those without any environmental benefits.

Responding to this new international climate of concern, national governments began to back away from aggressive biofuels promotion. In 2008, Brazil cut back on exports of sugar-based ethanol and China capped its use of cereals in biofuel production. Then, in 2011, the U.S. Congress allowed tax credits for ethanol blenders and tariffs on imported ethanol to lapse. Later in 2011, French president Nicolas Sarkozy launched a campaign to discipline biofuels policies within the G20 forum, and in 2012, the EU Commission proposed a policy change that would reduce the crop-derived percentage of transport fuel from 10 percent in 2020 down to just 5 percent. It was not just a fear of driving up food prices that led to this weakening of government support for biofuels. By 2012 biofuels were also less attractive in the marketplace because petroleum prices had declined even as the crops used as feedstocks to produce biofuels remained expensive. In addition, the urge in the United States to promote biofuels on national security grounds—as a means to reduce dependence on foreign oil— was also undercut by increased production of domestic shale gas, which put the country on a path to greater energy independence, even without biofuels.

Have higher international prices become a permanent feature of food politics?

Economists disagree on this question. Most were surprised by the spike in 2007–2008, and then doubly surprised by the persistence of high international prices in 2010–2012. Even the financial crisis and recession in the United States, followed by a debt crisis and recession in Europe, had failed to bring prices back down to the historical trend level. Many concluded that "the era of cheap food is over" and that traditional expectations of falling food prices over the long term would have to be revised.

Others recalled an earlier interlude of very high international food prices in the 1970s, one that led to similar pronouncements that the world had entered a new era. In 1971–1974, the price of both wheat and corn on the world market more than doubled, and the price of soybeans rose so high that even the United States briefly imposed an export ban. In November 1974, *Time* magazine branded this a "world food crisis" and asserted that hunger and famine were ravaging "hundreds of millions of the poorest citizens in at least 40 nations."

This earlier food price spike exhibited a number of characteristics similar to the spike of 2008. Then, just as in 2008, the price of all commodities, not just food, spiked upward. The macroeconomic explanation on that occasion was inflationary growth linked to lax monetary policies by the Federal Reserve Board in the United States. (In 2008 as well, the Federal Reserve Board cut interest rates to record low levels.) Also, just as in 2008, this earlier spike in international food prices was made worse by trade restrictions. In addition to a temporary U.S. embargo on soybean sales, Argentina, Brazil, Thailand, Myanmar (then Burma), and the European Union (then the Common Market) restricted food exports, stabilizing prices at home but destabilizing international market prices. Also in the 1970s, just as in 2008, food riots broke out in urban neighborhoods. The FAO hosted a global conference in Rome in 1974 to address the crisis, and U.S. Secretary of State Henry Kissinger called for action to ensure that within 10 years no child would have to go to bed hungry. Parallel calls to action were heard at a 2008 FAO conference in Rome. One danger today is that these much-needed new investments in agriculture will be put on the shelf if international food prices fall back down, which is what happened after the 1974 panic subsided.

The price spike of 1974 was brought to an end by a slow-down in economic growth worldwide, particularly following a tightening of U.S. monetary policy. By 1981, international food prices had dropped, and an erroneous conclusion was drawn that the world was once again well fed. In fact, then—just as now—the level of international food prices was a poor indicator of actual nutrition outcomes. It was the world recession and debt crisis of the 1980s, not the high international food prices of the 1970s, that caused the greatest human hardship. More people went hungry *after* the international price of food fell, during the economic recession years that followed. So it was only when the publicly declared food crisis ended in the 1980s that a more acute real food crisis began.

Consumption adjustments are made when international food prices spike upward, but most are made in rich countries rather than poor countries because the rich are the heaviest users of international markets. In international corn markets, for example, the biggest importer is Japan, and the biggest exporter is the United States, so when international corn prices go up these rich countries make the biggest adjustments. Typically, the first adjustment will be to feed less corn to farm animals such as chickens, pigs, and cattle. In wealthy countries, the fact that a great deal of grain is fed to animals actually provides a buffer against price fluctuations for food. In 1974, when corn prices more than doubled, the United States reduced the feeding of grain to livestock by 25 percent, which freed up more grain for direct consumption as food. Then as now, herd sizes were cut, eventually leading to higher meat prices and reduced meat consumption in wealthy societies. With obesity a growing health concern today, higher meat prices may not be an entirely bad outcome.

4

THE POLITICS OF CHRONIC HUNGER AND FAMINE

How do we measure hunger?

In our personal lives, hunger is a sensation we feel regularly at mealtime. In the world of politics and public policy, "hunger" is often used as a substitute word for chronic undernutrition, a long-term dietary condition that includes either a protein-energy deficit, a micronutrient deficit, or both. A protein-energy deficit occurs when the intake of calories falls consistently below what the human body burns. A micronutrient deficit occurs when the body does not get enough critical vitamins or minerals, such as iron, zinc, iodine, or vitamin A.

The visible indications of a protein-energy deficit include stunting (a low height relative to age), wasting (a low weight relative to height), and underweight (a low weight relative to age). All of these conditions can have serious medical consequences, particularly if they begin in the early months of life before age two. Inadequate early nutrition can lead to reduced cognition plus increased susceptibility to infectious disease and is a major cause of infant mortality. In the poorly fed regions of Africa, children under five die four times as often as in today's rich countries. Globally, some 3.5 million deaths per year among young children can be traced to protein-energy undernutrition.

When measuring children for size and weight, one complicating factor is that human stature and body size are influenced by genetics as well as nutrition, so small stature does not always reflect ill health; some children can be "small but healthy." Nonetheless, adverse long-term health effects have been confirmed statistically for populations in which large numbers of individuals are of below-average stature. Diets that provide abundant early access to protein, calcium, and vitamins A and D are known to improve both stature and health. As diets have improved around the world, in fact, people have grown not just more healthy but taller as well. In the United States today, compared to a century ago, the average adult male is three inches taller while enjoying a significantly longer life expectancy.

How many people around the world remain chronically undernourished?

The United Nations Food and Agriculture Organization (FAO) is tasked with estimating the total number of chronically undernourished people worldwide. These estimates are based on incomplete data, crude assumptions, and a methodology that sometimes changes, so they are often criticized for their imprecision. The FAO generates its estimates country by country, based on rough calculations such as the total availability of food in each country, the demographic structure of the population, the distribution of food access within the population (calculated when possible from nationally representative household surveys), and an assumed level of daily dietary energy (1,800 calories) required to provide adequate nutrition.

Using this method, the FAO has estimated most recently that the world in 2010–2012 contained 868 million undernourished people, or about 12 percent of the total world population at that time, which was significantly below the 16 percent level that prevailed in 1990.

Trends in aggregate numbers are difficult to agree on, but there is little controversy over where most undernourished people can be found. In 2012, the FAO concluded that only 2 percent of hungry people lived in the developed world. The rest lived in the developing world, with 35 percent in South Asia, 27 percent in Sub-Saharan Africa, 7 percent in Southeast Asia, and 6 percent in Latin America and the Caribbean. Parallel estimates made by other organizations such as the U.S. Department of Agriculture (USDA) and the International Food Policy Research Institute (IFPRI) agree that South Asia and Sub-Saharan Africa are where most of the world's undernourished people live.

All crude estimates of global hunger tend to underestimate micronutrient deficiencies, which are called "hidden hunger" because they are so often unseen. For example, a lack of iron in the diet tends to escape direct observation, yet the World Health Organization (WHO) estimates that in the developing world more than 40 percent of pregnant women do not get enough iron, leading to anemia, a risk factor for hemorrhage and death in childbirth.

The most reliable method for judging trends in global hunger is to focus not on entire populations but instead on children under five years of age, a cohort that is both highly vulnerable and often easier for clinicians to monitor. Among children, nutrition has steadily been improving around the world. In July 2012, the School of Public Health at Imperial College, London, using the most recent data on children's height and weight in 141 developing countries, found that the proportion of children classified as moderately to severely underweight had fallen from 30 percent in 1985 to 19 percent in 2011. The prevalence of moderate to severe stunting (low height for age) had declined from 47 percent to 30 percent. Some large countries such as China saw particularly dramatic improvements, and in rapidly growing Brazil the proportion of underweight children had fallen by half in a single decade. In Chile, the proportion of underweight children had fallen essentially zero by

2011. Regionally, about half of the world's underweight children still lived in South Asia, mostly in India. In Sub-Saharan Africa, the undernourished share of the population actually increased between 1985 and the mid-1990s, but then average height and weight outcomes finally began to improve there as well.

What causes chronic undernutrition?

The persistence of chronic undernutrition usually reflects a persistence of deep poverty, and it usually goes away when poverty goes away. Household surveys in Burundi, Ghana, Kenya, and Malawi show that more than 90 percent of those still classified as poor (living on less than $1 a day) were also "hungry," with daily energy intake below 2,200 calories or a diet lacking in essential diversity. In Bangladesh, 74 percent of those classified as poor are also hungry. In addition to poverty, other risk factors for chronic undernutrition include living in remote rural areas, having fewer years of schooling, and lacking secure access to land.

Hunger risks also increase with low social status and political marginalization. Other things being equal, ethnic minorities are more likely to be hungry. For example, in Sri Lanka, Indian Tamils are at a disadvantage. In Central America, stunting is twice as widespread among indigenous children compared to non-indigenous children, and in South Asia, hill tribes and "scheduled castes" suffer greater nutrition deficits than others. In Africa, female-headed households are more at risk. The least well-fed individuals in many societies are orphans and street children.

Urban poverty is highly visible to those who visit developing countries, yet it is poverty in the countryside that usually generates the larger share of chronic undernutrition. There are roughly twice as many poor and hungry people in the African countryside compared to urban areas, and in South Asia the ratio is three to one. This greater prevalence of hunger in rural areas represents a cruel paradox: rural dwellers usually produce food for a living, yet they are often the first not to get enough for themselves. This is because in South Asia and Africa many rural dwellers are either landless agricultural laborers, working only seasonally and for low pay, or they are impoverished smallholder farmers who may have access to land but lack the tools needed (irrigation, improved seeds, fertilizers) to make their labor productive. They work all day and waste nothing, but the food and money often run out before the next harvest. They are "efficient but poor," living in what development economists describe as a "poverty trap."

Does chronic hunger trigger political unrest?

Food price spikes can cause social protests, but chronic undernutrition is seldom a trigger for political change. It should be, but it is not. Persistently poor and hungry communities seldom have the means to threaten governments. A preponderance of the hungry will usually be young children and illiterate women located in remote rural settings, typically lacking political knowledge or organization. Often they will be from disadvantaged castes or from marginalized racial and ethnic groups. They may also be governed by non-democratic political regimes in which a single ruling party, a single dynastic family, the military, or a theocracy of religious clerics will hold all the power. In systems such as these, it is usually safe for governments to ignore poor and hungry people in the countryside.

As mentioned in Chapter 3, physical hunger and undernutrition were not the cause of the "Arab Spring" street demonstrations that toppled governments in Tunisia, Libya, and Egypt in 2011. In urban Tunisia, where the demonstrations began (over issues of government corruption, unemployment, and personal dignity), chronic undernutrition was hard to find. In all of Tunisia, only 2.9 percent of children under five were underweight, which was less than one-fifth the global average of 16.2 percent. None of the food protests of 2008 and none of the Arab Spring protests of 2011 broke out in a country that had fallen into the IFPRI "extremely alarming" global hunger index category. If physical hunger were a leading source of political instability, it would be rural rather than urban populations leading the demonstrations, and governments (to ensure their survival) would be investing more in rural agricultural development.

Is chronic undernutrition a problem in the United States?

In the United States, the top problem linked to diet is obesity, not undernutrition. This represents a dramatic change from the middle years of the twentieth century, when deep poverty in America generated widespread undernutrition. The United States today still has many communities living in poverty relative to average national wealth and income, but today's poor are far less likely to under-consume food.

One full century ago, when the average consumer income in the United States was only one-fourth as high as today, and when the price of most basic food commodities was twice as high in real terms, getting enough to eat was a serious problem for large parts of the population. At the beginning of the twentieth century, the average American spent 41 percent of personal income on food (compared to just 10 percent today) and low-income Americans often could not afford a healthy diet. During the hard times of the Great Depression in the 1930s, several thousand Americans died each year from diseases such as pellagra (niacin deficiency), beriberi (thiamin deficiency), rickets (vitamin D deficiency), and scurvy (vitamin C deficiency). In 1938, over 20 percent of preschool children in America had rickets, with hundreds dying from this crippling ailment.

During the second half of the twentieth century, such deficits were steadily overcome, thanks to a decline in absolute poverty, a continued decline in food commodity prices, plus a new set of government-funded anti-hunger interventions. A National School Lunch Act was passed by Congress in 1946, partly in reaction to the poor nutritional status that had been discovered among young men drafted into service early in World War II. Then in the 1960s, following media reports of scandalous poverty and hunger in rural Appalachia, a federal Food Stamp program designed to help low-income families purchase a nutritionally adequate diet was expanded dramatically. Then in the 1970s, a Special Supplemental Nutrition Program for Women, Infants, and Children (the WIC program) was created to improve the health of low-income pregnant women, new mothers, infants, and young children at nutritional risk.

These interventions produced gratifying results, but at a greatly expanded cost to taxpayers in recent years. In 2011, the federal government spent $78 billion on the SNAP (food stamp) program alone, up from about $30 billion in 2007. Partly this reflected the 2008 financial crisis and recession, which pushed more families into poverty, making them eligible for SNAP benefits. In order to be eligible for SNAP, a household must have a low income (e.g., at or below $24,000 a year, for a three-person family) plus total assets below a certain limit. The average monthly benefit in 2012 was $133 per person, with roughly 45 percent of all recipients being children.

SNAP spending has also grown because of a change in the law in 1996 allowing individual states to lower the eligibility requirements and to make more aggressive efforts to enroll eligible residents, which they now do as a way to channel more federal money to their communities. A switch was also made late in the 1990s allowing benefits to be delivered through an EBT card that could be discreetly swiped at checkout, rather than through the redemption of paper coupons, which reduced the public stigma associated with being on food stamps. One result was a significant increase in participation rates. In 2001, only about half of those eligible participated, but by 2011, three-quarters of those eligible were receiving benefits. Roughly 15 percent of Americans are now on SNAP.

Often only a small share of the food purchases made through SNAP are additional to purchases that people would make anyway. Poor households typically use the benefit to replace some existing cash expenditures on food so as to allocate more cash to other things such as housing, clothing, health, and education. In this way the SNAP program functions as an important income supplement and insurance program for the poor. This evolution of the program has made it a target for welfare critics; House Budget Committee Chair Paul Ryan (R., Wis.) proposes turning SNAP into a block grant program, a move that would likely lead to cuts.

Partly thanks to programs like SNAP and WIC, poverty in America today is far less likely to result in undernutrition. Comparing poor children to middle-class children in America, the average consumption of protein, vitamins, and minerals has become virtually identical for both groups, and average calorie consumption for both groups is now comparably excessive. According to the WHO, the percentage of American children suffering from moderate or severe wasting in 2003–2008 was zero. The percentage who suffered from severe underweight was also zero. As for micronutrient deficits, the Centers for Disease Control and Prevention found in its most recent report that only 10 percent of the general U.S. population was deficient in vitamin B6, vitamin D, and iron, and less than 1 percent was deficient in folate, vitamin A, and vitamin E.

Advocacy groups that campaign against hunger in America seldom celebrate these dramatic achievements, perhaps fearing that a declaration of victory would de-motivate the food assistance interventions that helped to bring it about. Hunger advocacy organizations prefer instead to cite survey data from the U.S. Department of Agriculture that measure not clinical undernutrition but instead a subjective condition of "food insecurity," based on such factors as worrying at least once during the previous 12 months about running out of food, or perhaps not eating for a whole day because there wasn't enough money for food. Using these more relaxed standards, the USDA reported in 2011 that 14.9 percent of all U.S. households were "food insecure," and 5.7 percent had "very low food security." A careful reading of the data reveals, however, that *on an average day*, only 0.8–1.1 percent of U.S. households experienced very low food security in 2011.

Do developing countries have policy remedies for chronic undernutrition?

Many middle-income developing countries also operate nutrition-oriented "safety net" programs for the poor. One of the most successful in recent years has been Brazil, where President Lula da Silva launched a Zero Hunger (Fome Zero) program in January 2003. As of 2006, according to the FAO, this program had reduced the nation's undernourished population from 17 million to 11.9 million. Achieving this success required a continuing outlay of significant public resources, just as with SNAP in the United States.

Brazil's strategy initially included a $400 million conditional cash transfer (Food Card) program to supplement the income of poor families buying more food (the cash transfers were conditioned on school attendance and health checkups); a $130 million program to purchase food from family farmers (PAA); a $65 million health and nutrition program for the elderly, children, and nursing mothers to address illnesses caused by vitamin and micronutrient deficiencies; an expanded school feeding program; a program to monitor food intake; a food and nutrition education program; and a food supply and distribution program targeting low-income populations in larger cities. In 2009, so-called Family Grants benefiting 12.4 million families replaced Food Cards, at a greatly expanded annual cost to the state of $6.5 billion. These Family Grants in 2009 represented 2 percent of Brazil's federal budget but only 0.4 percent of GDP. Less prosperous countries are not able to afford such programs, and countries with less administrative capacity are not able to implement them properly.

Brazil's programs have paid off in terms of improved health and nutrition outcomes. In the city of Guaribas, the Food Card program helped to end infant deaths attributable to malnutrition and to expand vaccine coverage from 9 to 96 percent and prenatal care from 10 to 80 percent. The Fome Zero program's biggest challenge has always been striking a balance between doing enough to reach all of the poor, versus doing so much as to discourage private investments in the delivery of market-based nutrition and health services. Local Management Committees help ensure appropriate targeting of public assistance by scrutinizing local Cadastro Unico (Unified Registers) of those in extreme poverty.

Governments elsewhere in the developing world have implemented food subsidy programs that are less well administered and less well targeted. One approach is to set up a parallel food supply system for the poor in which citizens holding ration cards can go to "fair price shops" to purchase cheap bread or flour. India has operated such a system for decades, but management is poor and waste and corruption are rampant. Another approach is to flood urban markets with government-purchased grain, a method often used to excess in Egypt. This approach is costly to the government, it makes food artificially cheap for all urban dwellers, not just the poor, and it often fails to reach rural areas where needs are greatest. Food safety net programs are nominally intended to improve nutrition, but their deeper motivation is also to deliver benefits to politically powerful urban groups, such as civil servants, policemen, and labor unions.

Micronutrient deficits can also be addressed by policy interventions in the developing world, often through the "fortification" of wheat flour with iron, folic acid, or vitamin B, usually at centralized industrial milling facilities. This is a relatively inexpensive process (it adds only a tiny fraction of a penny to the cost of a loaf of bread) and effective for those who get the fortified flour, but once again it can exclude the rural economy, where milling is small scale and localized.

Supporting broadly based income growth has always been the best long-run approach for reducing chronic undernutrition in developing countries. In the poorest agricultural societies, in Asia and Africa, this will require in the first instance an increase in the productivity of small farmers. So long as agricultural labor earns only about $1 a day, the vast majority of rural citizens who work as farmers will remain poor and hence vulnerable to chronic undernutrition. According to the World Bank, rural poverty and hunger worsened in Sub-Saharan Africa in the 1980s and 1990s largely because the average annual value added of farm labor was low and falling (from $418 in 1980, to just $379 by 1997). Meanwhile, hunger was in decline in East Asia because average value added per farm worker was increasing sharply, up by 50 percent in Thailand and up by 100 percent in China. Increasing the productivity of farm labor typically requires the introduction of new technologies such as improved seeds, fertilizers, and machinery. It also requires government investment in basic rural public goods such as roads and electricity. Because governments in Africa have made few such investments, farm productivity remains low and large numbers remain poor and hungry.

What is the difference between undernutrition and famine?

A famine takes place when large numbers of people die quickly in a specific location because they have not had enough food to eat. Some die from actual starvation—acute wasting—while others die from diseases that attack people who are in a weakened state.

The United Nations officially declares a famine based on three criteria: at least 20 percent of households in an area must face extreme food shortages and a limited ability to cope; the acute malnutrition rate must exceed 30 percent; and the death rate must exceed two persons per day per 10,000 people in the population. While low food intake still afflicts hundreds of millions of poor people in the developing world, actual famines have fortunately become rare.

When have famines taken place?

Famine is as old as recorded history. In the book of Revelation, famine is represented as one of the four horsemen of the Apocalypse. Europe suffered a great famine in 1315–1317 that killed millions. In France during the Hundred Years' War (1337–1453), a combination of warfare, crop failures, and epidemics reduced the population by two-thirds. In Ireland in 1845–1849, famine triggered by a recurring potato blight killed 1 million people outright and drove another million from the country as refugees. In India, there were 14 famines between the eleventh and seventeenth centuries, and India's great famine of 1876–1878 killed 6 to 10 million people.

By the twentieth century, famine had largely disappeared from western Europe, but it continued to appear in Asia, Africa, and also in eastern Europe. In the Soviet Union under Lenin and Stalin, the Ukraine experienced one famine in 1921–1922, then a more severe one in 1932–1933. During World War II, the city of Leningrad suffered a famine that killed roughly 1 million people. In Asia, a famine visited Bengal in 1943 and killed 1.5 to 3 million people. Starvation devastated China in 1958–1961, during Mao Zedong's disastrous Great Leap Forward, killing as many as 30 million people, the single largest famine of all time. A famine began in North Korea in 1996, and to a lesser extent it may continue to the present day, with a death toll impossible for outsiders to estimate, given the closed nature of that state. In Africa, famine struck in the Sahel and in Ethiopia in the early 1970s and then again in Ethiopia and Sudan in the 1980s. Most recently, a famine was formally declared in southern Somalia in 2011.

What causes famines?

Famines have diverse causes. In some instances, a natural event is the trigger, such as the drought in the African Sahel in the early 1970s that devastated both grain production and the forage needed for animals. In other cases (Ireland in 1845), a crop disease—in this case, a potato blight—can wipe out staple food production. In still other cases, such as Bangladesh in 1974, it can be rain-induced flooding, which disrupts agricultural production and drives food prices in the market beyond the reach of the poor. In Ethiopia, Sudan, and Mozambique in the 1980s, adverse impacts from drought were compounded by violent internal conflict. In the Russian city of Leningrad in 1941, famine broke out when a surrounding German army laid siege.

Ideology also can cause famine. In Ukraine in 1932–1933, Stalin took land and food away from private farmers because he viewed them as "capitalist" enemies of the working class. There was no drought, no blight, no flood, and no war—just a coercive government takeover intended to "socialize" the farming sector. Peasants who resisted were imprisoned or shot. As production fell, forcible state procurements of grain continued, and at least 6 million people starved—in one of the richest grain-growing regions of the world. More than ideological blindness may have been at work; historian Robert Conquest, author of *Harvest of Sorrow*, has depicted these events as a "terror famine," an intentional campaign to starve Ukrainians suspected of political disloyalty to Moscow.

The famine in China in 1959–1961 was also driven by ideology—in this case, a 1958 decision by Mao Zedong to organize food production (and everything else) according to a system of people's communes. Ownership of farmland and control over grain harvests were both taken away, which eliminated any incentive for farmers to be productive. Peasant farmers also had their labor burdened by a new requirement that they begin producing steel out of scrap metal in "backyard furnaces." When grain production collapsed in 1959, requirements by local Communist Party cadres to deliver grain to the state to feed the urban workforce were nonetheless enforced, and even increased. This left the peasants with nothing for themselves, and 15 to 30 million starved. In 1962, Mao was finally forced to abandon most of the policies that were causing the famine.

Despite this wide variety of famine causes, some scholars have tried to offer generalized explanations. The most prominent modern famine scholar is Amartya Sen, a Bengali economist and philosopher who won a Nobel Prize in 1998 for his contribution to welfare economics. Sen, who witnessed the famine in Bengal in 1943 as a young boy, wrote an important book in 1981 (*Poverty and Famines: An Essay on Entitlement and Deprivation*) challenging the conventional belief that famines are caused by "food availability declines." Sen had found that during the 1943 Bengal famine, locally available food supplies did not decline; the deprivation resulted instead from a surge in wartime spending by Great Britain (which had colonized Bengal and was then fighting Japan), triggering a pattern of panic buying and hoarding that drove the price of food out of the reach of the poor. As many as 3 million died, even though the total quantity of food available had never declined.

Sen explains a 1974 Bangladesh famine in much the same way. Floods disrupted agricultural labor, which in turn cut the income of landless farmworkers. The floods also created an *expectation* of rice shortages, which caused hoarding and panic buying, finally driving prices out of the reach of the poor. Vulnerable groups that depended on a particular relationship between the market value of their own labor and the market price of rice found that their *exchange entitlement* (Sen's terminology) to food had been taken away. Those with a more direct entitlement to food—for example, those owning the land that produced the food—did not starve.

Sen's warnings of famine dangers linked to unregulated markets remain popular, yet his own later work shifted the emphasis to a concern regarding undemocratic political systems. Sen observed that famines did not tend to occur in democratic political systems, where leaders know they will be punished in the next election if they allow their own people to starve. Democratic India avoided famine in 1965 and

1966, despite two consecutive years of failing monsoon rains, because the leadership turned to the outside world for millions of tons of emergency food aid and expanded its public food distribution systems. Non-democratic China provided no such response when the Great Leap failed, and it even covered up its famine from the outside world. At the extreme, states lacking both free elections and free markets—such as China under Mao, or North Korea today—will be the most famine-prone.

How do famines end?

Famines can end for nearly as many different reasons as they begin. In the case of Ireland, famine deaths declined in part because many fled the country (including a large emigration to the United States) and also because so many potential victims had already died. In addition, Britain finally responded by sending food and funds to help Ireland, so by 1849–1850, public workhouses were able to care for those left destitute by the continuing crop failures.

In the case of Ukraine in 1933, roughly 25 percent of the population eventually perished, including nearly all of the propertied farmers who had resisted the move toward socialized agriculture. Once private agriculture had been destroyed and Stalin's political objectives achieved, he reduced mandatory state procurements from the region and allowed food distribution to resume, so the famine subsided. In the case of the Bengal famine of 1943, the crisis ended when the government in London finally accepted the need to import 1 million tons of grain to Bengal, to discourage hoarding and bring food prices back down to a level the poor could afford. In the case of Mao's famine in China, the abandonment of the Great Leap policies, a decision to permit grain imports, and a reduction in mandatory state procurements were all key to ending the starvation. In the case of the African Sahel, surviving pastoralist populations first relocated southward to less drought-prone regions, and then, fortunately, the cyclical rains improved. In the case of Ethiopia, Sudan, and Mozambique in the 1980s, famines that were largely triggered by drought and civil conflict ended when the rains returned or the civil conflicts diminished.

What has been the most successful international response to famine?

The best international response to famine is to deliver food and medical aid, but not too soon and not for too long. If international food aid is distributed too soon at feeding stations in rural market towns after a drought, some people who are not yet starving will be tempted to leave their farms and relocate to these feeding stations in search of free food, water, and medicine. If they stay, these farmers will then be away from their fields when the rains return the next season and will not be in a position to plant a new crop. They will become permanently dependent on food aid. Dislocations of this kind need to be avoided as long as food-stressed populations are still "coping."

Fortunately, a wide range of coping strategies are usually available in impoverished countries when temporary food shortages loom, including eating fewer meals every day, switching to less desirable "famine foods" (including wild foods that can be foraged or hunted in the bush), and selling off some animals or some nonessential household assets, such as jewelry, to raise the money needed to purchase food. Only when people run out of such options and begin taking more drastic steps, such as selling off essential farm implements, should they be encouraged to relocate to feeding camps, and even then they should be kept in this dependent condition only as long as necessary. Once the rains return or once the violent conflict ends, internally displaced people should return to their farming communities. This can be encouraged by replacing the food aid with a one-time distribution of farm implements, animals, and cash—the things that people will need to return to a productive livelihood.

Can famine be prevented?

Famines are now prevented on a regular basis. In Africa today, even large-scale drought does not have to result in famine. After a series of traumatizing emergencies in the 1970s and 1980s, the international community fortunately set in place for Africa a famine early warning system (FEWS) based on regular assessments of local rainfall patterns and market prices to ensure a more effective response to future drought emergencies.

This system, operated by the UN Food and Agriculture Organization (FAO) and the U.S. Agency for International Development (USAID), proved effective in giving advance warning of food aid needs when drought struck southern Africa in 1991–1992. In Malawi, Namibia, Swaziland, and Zimbabwe, cereal production fell 60–70 percent, and throughout the region, 17–20 million people were placed at starvation risk. Yet, thanks to an effective food aid response from the UN World Food Programme (WFP) working in cooperation with local governments and humanitarian relief non-governmental organizations (NGOs), the only famine deaths reported were in Mozambique, where aid was impossible to deliver because of an ongoing civil war. The new international capacity to prevent famine in Africa was then successfully tested a second time in southern Africa in 2001–2002, when drought returned and 15 million people were put at starvation risk. Once again, the international food aid response was timely, and essentially, no famine deaths occurred.

This new international famine-prevention capacity can falter, however, in countries torn by internal conflict. In 2011 the Horn of Africa experienced the worst recorded drought in 60 years, and millions were placed at risk in Ethiopia, Kenya, Djibouti, and Somalia. The international community responded with a vigorous famine prevention operation, operated once again by the World Food Programme. Famine was avoided everywhere except southern Somalia, where 50,000 to 100,000 people died. Famine deaths occurred because southern

Somalia was under the control of al Shabaab, an armed jihadist militia group loyal to al Qaeda that refused to let food aid come in.

In the modern era, we can conclude, natural disasters alone do not cause famine. When famines occur, it is because armed groups (or national governments, in the case of North Korea) intentionally block famine relief.

5

FOOD AID AND AGRICULTURAL DEVELOPMENT ASSISTANCE

What is international food aid?

Food aid is the international shipment of food through "concessional" channels, as a gift, rather than through commercial channels, as a sale. The food can be given by a donor government to a recipient government, by a donor government to a non-governmental organization (NGO) working inside the recipient country, or through a multilateral organization such as the World Food Programme (WFP) of the United Nations. The food can be sourced from a government-owned surplus supply, or purchased in the home market of the donor country, purchased from a local market in the recipient country, or purchased in a third-country market close to the recipient country. The purpose of the food aid can be to address a temporary famine emergency, to cushion higher food prices (as during the 2008 world food crisis), to feed a dependent refugee population, or to support local work or education activities (through "food for work" programs, or school lunch programs). It can generate cash income for assistance organizations through sales into a local market (called monetization), it can dispose of a surplus, and in some cases it can be used to reward recipient governments for taking foreign policy actions pleasing to the donor government. Because there are so many ways to give food aid and so many different reasons for giving it, generalizations about this policy instrument are almost always dangerous.

There is one exception: food aid today can safely be described as less important to the world food system than it was in the past. As a share of all cross-border food shipments, food aid is no longer of great significance. In the early 1970s, international food aid still made up about 10 percent of all cross-border food flows, but food aid declined in relative importance as commercial trade expanded, and now it makes up only about 3 percent of total cross-border food flows. Food aid does, however, remain a significant share of total food imports for some individual recipient countries.

Which countries get food aid?

The answer to this question has changed over time. In the early 1950s, the most important recipients of international food aid were in Europe and East Asia. Most of the food came from the United States to support reconstruction in these regions following the damage of World War II, for example through the Marshall Plan. By the 1960s, the direction of most food aid had shifted toward South Asia, especially India. Then, in the 1970s and 1980s, a great deal of American food aid went first to Vietnam and then to the Middle East, largely in service of foreign policy objectives. Finally, by the 1990s, Sub-Saharan Africa had emerged as the target destination of most food aid. According to one United Nations Food and Agriculture Organization (FAO) report in the 1990s, concessional international food aid provided more than 40 percent of total cereal imports for more than 40 recipient countries, and most of those countries were in Africa. Roughly 60 percent of all international food aid now goes to Sub-Saharan Africa.

Food aid today moves less through bilateral government-to-government channels and more through the UN World

Food Programme. This change took place after an important UN World Food Conference in 1974, partly in response to the international food price crisis of that decade. By 2000, roughly 38 percent of all global food aid was delivered by the WFP, and by 2009, 64 percent of food aid was delivered through such multilateral channels. National governments in rich countries still fund nearly all food aid, but more than 90 percent of this aid is now distributed either by the WFP or by NGOs, rather than from government to government.

The enlarged role of the WFP, a politically neutral UN agency, has helped to diminish the role of crude favoritism based on foreign policy calculations in determining who gets aid and who does not. Unfortunately, this has made it easier for some recipient countries to grow comfortable depending on food aid. In the 1960s, when most food aid came straight from the U.S. government, often with diplomatic and foreign policy strings attached, recipient countries such as India became uncomfortable with the relationship and, partly to escape a dependence on food aid, made larger investments in their own agricultural production. Governments in Africa today that depend on food aid have shown less urgency in reducing their dependence because the food comes to them from the United Nations without any political conditions.

Do rich countries give food aid to dispose of their surplus production?

This was true for the United States in the 1950s, when farm subsidy policies had generated a surplus quantity of wheat, which the government had to buy from farmers. One way to get this surplus out of government storage bins was international food aid. Under Public Law 480, enacted in 1954, also known as the Food for Peace program, government-owned surplus commodities could be shipped directly to recipient governments in the developing world. To respect the sensitivities of recipient countries, as well as to avoid complaints of unfair trade from export competitors, a "payment" for the food was accepted in the form of nonconvertible local currency that could only be spent by the U.S. embassy inside the local economy. Long-term and low-interest credit terms were also allowed, so the food was essentially given away free. The P.L. 480 program played a significant role in helping the U.S. government dispose of its grain surplus at a time when commercial export markets were weak. By 1960, fully 70 percent of U.S. wheat exports were moving abroad as concessional food aid rather than commercial sales.

Later in the 1960s, however, the United States began supporting domestic farm income with cash payments rather than through purchases of grain, so the amount of surplus food owned by the government dwindled. This might have brought an end to the food aid program, but by then it had become a convenient tool in the conduct of American foreign policy, so P.L. 480 did not disappear. Government-owned grain surpluses were gone by the 1970s, but Congress authorized the continuation of the food aid program based on purchases of food in the marketplace, as long as it was purchased in the United States and then shipped abroad in U.S. vessels.

Why are America's food aid policies so difficult to change?

America's method of giving food aid has changed little since the 1970s. To the present day, most of the food is purchased in the United States, and most of it is shipped in U.S. vessels. It would cost taxpayers less to purchase the food closer to the site of the emergency, and every other donor country, including the European countries, Japan, and now even Canada, has moved toward local purchase as the best practice for food aid, but rules set by Congress have prevented the United States from doing the same.

Changing these rules will not be easy. In 2006 and 2007, President George W. Bush attempted to allocate a small percentage of the food aid budget for procurements abroad, but

Congress said no. Former president Bill Clinton said that it was to Bush's "everlasting credit" that he had at least challenged Congress on local purchase. In 2012, the U.S. Agency for International Development (USAID) revised its rules to allow local purchase for assistance goods other than food, but the rules for food aid were made by Congress, not the USAID administrator. In 2013, when President Barack Obama called once again for a move to allow locally purchased food aid, more than 60 domestic organizations, led by farm lobby and maritime lobby groups, signed a letter to Congress objecting to such a change.

A second distinctive trait of United States food aid policy is called "cargo preference," which is a legal requirement that most food aid be shipped in U.S.-flag vessels, which are 70 to 80 percent more costly per ton than foreign-flag carriers. The Department of Defense joins the shipping lobby in favoring this provision. This is because it allegedly helps keep an American merchant fleet in operation to provide secure ocean transport in the event of a future military conflict. In 2012, Congress reduced this "cargo preference" requirement from 75 percent to 50 percent, but the maritime lobby has vowed to fight this reform. Because foreign purchase is not allowed and because so much shipment on U.S.-flag vessels is required, roughly 65 percent of America's food aid spending is eaten up by administrative and transport costs.

Another dubious feature of American food aid is the frequent practice of selling the food into local markets rather than targeting deliveries to needy recipients. Over one recent three-year period, more than $500 million worth of American food aid was "monetized" in this fashion. This practice lowers local food costs for the well-to-do as well as for the poor and hungry, and by undercutting market prices it can disadvantage local farmers, thus prolonging dependence on food aid. This practice persists because some of the American NGOs handling the food rely on the monetary proceeds from sales to fund their other local development projects. A number of leading American NGOs, including CARE, Oxfam, Catholic Relief Services, and Save the Children, have signed a declaration, along with British, French, and Canadian aid groups, calling this practice into question.

If Congress were to end monetization, allow food purchases to be made outside the United States, and eliminate cargo preference, each dollar spent through P.L. 480 would deliver significantly more food to needy recipients. Realistically, however, if these reforms were made, Congress would probably authorize many fewer dollars for the program. America's food aid program is the largest in the world (50 percent of all food aid globally comes from the United States) in part because Congress knows that there are benefits for domestic farmers, the shipping industry, American NGOs, and even national defense.

Does food aid create dependence or hurt farmers in recipient countries?

In the early days of food aid in the 1950s and 1960s, when large shipments of surplus grain were first sent to the developing world as food aid, critics warned that a costly and dangerous dependence might result. Local consumers would become hooked on cheap food delivered from abroad, and local farmers would go out of business due to depressed food prices in the marketplace. Some even suspected that this was the American farm lobby's intent. Once the recipients had been lured into a dependence on food aid, the aid would be taken away and they would be forced to graduate to the status of paying customers.

Agricultural lobby groups in the United States have often hoped that food aid would work in this manner as commercial export promotion, but it seldom has. America's largest food aid shipments in the past went to countries like Peru, Haiti, India, Indonesia, Vietnam, Jordan, Egypt, and the Philippines, and none of these later became a leading commercial market for U.S. agricultural sales. By some estimates, more than half of all food aid actually displaces purchased shipments, meaning it destroys more commercial sales in the short run than it ever creates in the long run. Some of the commercial sales displaced will be from competing exporters, so food aid is also a contentious issue in international trade. Where commercial sales do increase in the long run, it is usually a result of income growth in the recipient country leading to more food demand, implying that foreign investment and development assistance are actually far better tools for commercial export promotion than food aid.

Even as a subsidy to domestic farmers, food aid has limited benefit today because food aid shipments are now so small relative to commercial agricultural exports and total sales. In 2012, the USDA spent roughly $2 billion purchasing and shipping food aid. By comparison, total commercial agricultural exports from the United States were valued at $135 billion and total cash sales by farms at $385 billion. For some individual commodity groups such as wheat or rice growers, food aid shipments still make up a valued share of total sales, but for American agriculture as a whole the importance is now small.

There are some examples of food aid altering the behavior of consumers and food producers in recipient countries. Large deliveries of wheat and rice into West Africa in the 1970s accelerated local shifts in consumer demand away from sorghum and millet toward breads made from wheat. Large deliveries of maize as food aid to the Horn of Africa likewise encouraged recipients, many of them pastoralists, to shift their diet from animal products to grains. In most recipient countries, however, the quantity of food aid delivered has not been large enough inside the local market to trigger a significant shift in consumer behavior. Even in some of the poorest recipient countries, such as Ethiopia, only about one in ten local recipients ever receives enough food aid (in value terms) to equal more than one-quarter of individual income. Displaced communities who get food aid at refugee camps can develop a dangerous dependence on the handouts, but entire national populations do not.

As for local farmers, when unusually large quantities of food aid are delivered in an untargeted manner at the wrong time—for example, corresponding with a local harvest—damage can be done. Yet many poor local farmers are themselves purchasers of food during much of the year, so food aid deliveries that are well timed help them by keeping the local price of food down during the off season, when they have nothing to sell anyway. Still, there are instances when poorly timed or poorly targeted food aid did lead to local production disincentives, for example the large shipments of food aid that went to Russia in the 1990s when the cold war ended, or large shipments to Ethiopia in 1999–2000 that arrived at the wrong time and collapsed local sorghum prices. Such problems are better contained today because more food aid is delivered for humanitarian purposes rather than as crude surplus disposal, and it more often moves through multilateral humanitarian agencies or NGOs that incorporate targeting and price awareness into their programs.

Do governments seek coercive power from food aid?

Governments are sometimes tempted to seek a coercive advantage by manipulating—or threatening to manipulate—the volume and timing of food aid shipments. On one noted occasion in 1965–1968, President Lyndon Johnson gave in to this temptation in his dealings with India by conditioning the continued delivery of food aid on changes that he wanted to see in Indian agricultural policy, as well as reduced Indian criticism of Johnson's war policies in Vietnam. India had suffered two sequential harvest failures in 1965 and 1966 and was heavily dependent on deliveries of food aid wheat from the United States. It did agree to some of the agricultural policy changes that Johnson wanted, most of which were good for India in the end, but it was deeply resentful of the coercion and refused to end criticism of American policies in Vietnam. The final political outcome was intensified Indian hostility toward the United States, not compliant subservience.

Efforts to gain diplomatic leverage by manipulating commercial food exports are even more prone to fail. In 1980 President Jimmy Carter attempted to punish the Soviet Union for its invasion of Afghanistan with a partial embargo on U.S. commercial grain exports, mostly wheat and corn. Carter's hope was that reduced imports would oblige the Soviets to cut back on the feeding of grain to cattle and pigs, resulting in meat shortages that might then reduce internal support for the Communist regime. The U.S. embargo failed when other grain-exporting countries—particularly Argentina, Australia, and Canada—agreed to sell more to the Soviets to make up for the U.S. sales being blocked. The Soviets, by offering only small price premiums to these other suppliers, were able to import roughly the same total quantity of grain during the U.S. embargo as they had imported before the embargo. They meanwhile made the most of the embargo by blaming some meat shortages (which they were going to experience anyway) on Jimmy Carter.

Food is hard to withhold for coercive purposes in part because most governments do not want to be blamed for imposing humanitarian hardships on foreign populations. In recent negotiations with North Korea over food aid, the United States has paradoxically found itself at a disadvantage because any withdrawal of food aid could be depicted by the North as an American effort to use starvation as a tool of foreign policy, an accusation that the United States wishes to avoid.

How is agricultural development assistance different from food aid?

Sending free food to poor countries is a valuable and lifesaving step in short-run circumstances, but the recipient countries would do better in the long run to develop the potential of their own farmers to supply food. Most farmers in poor countries are producing far below their potential. For example, according to the Consultative Group on International Agricultural Research (CGIAR), average cereal yields in Africa are only about 1 ton per hectare, compared to 2.5 tons in South Asia and 4.5 tons in East Asia. If governments in Africa gave farmers access to better technologies (seeds, fertilizers, machinery), better training through schooling and extension services, and better rural infrastructures to provide roads, water, and electrical power, the region's dependence on food aid could quickly be ended. Agricultural development assistance is a form of "foreign aid" intended to help poor countries bring these vital assets to their own farmers.

Agricultural development assistance is difficult for politicians in rich countries to support because it does not produce instantly visible benefits. Food aid supporters, by contrast, can provide photographs of refugee children whose lives are being saved by food deliveries. Most agricultural development programs, such as investments in agricultural research or agricultural education, do not deliver their full pay off for a decade or more, and even then the benefit will be difficult to document.

Economists using the best measurement techniques available have nonetheless found large long-term gains from agricultural development investments. In the developing world as a whole, the International Food Policy Research Institute in 2000 calculated a median rate of return of 48 percent for investments in agricultural research and a 63 percent return for investments in extension. Even in difficult settings such as Africa the returns are high. The World Bank's *World Development Report 2008* documented rates of return on agricultural research in Africa that averaged 35 percent per year, accompanied by significant reductions in poverty. The International Food Policy Research Institute (IFPRI) has estimated 50 percent average rates of return when the spending goes through Africa's own national agricultural research systems (NARS).

Investments in rural infrastructure also have large payoffs in the long run. In India, according to calculations done by IFPRI, investments in rural roads were even more powerful than investments in agricultural research for the purpose of lifting people out of poverty. Similar impacts have been measured in Africa. One IFPRI study in 2004 found that spending on rural feeder roads in Uganda had better than a 7 to 1 ratio of benefits (in terms of agricultural growth and rural poverty reduction) relative to costs. Supporters of agricultural development assistance believe that rich countries should use their foreign assistance programs to help poor countries make investments of this kind in rural infrastructure and agricultural research.

How much international assistance do rich countries provide for agricultural development?

In 2008–2009, the Organisation for Economic Co-operation and Development (OECD) in Paris calculated that the world's rich countries, in combination, provided $9 billion in annual assistance to agriculture, two-thirds of that through bilateral channels, and one-third through multilateral channels such as the World Bank, the European Union (EU), and the International Fund for Agricultural Development (IFAD). The largest share of this assistance went to Sub-Saharan Africa, and the second-largest share to South Asia. One-quarter of the aid went for direct efforts to boost agricultural production, about one-fifth went to support changes in agricultural policies, and smaller amounts went for agricultural education and research, rural development, and agricultural water resources.

The international food price spike of 2008 then stimulated an overdue effort by rich countries to increase these outlays. It was noticed that, in real terms, international assistance to agriculture in 2009 was actually 30 percent lower than it had been in the mid-1980s. A new political effort was made by development assistance advocates to return spending to the earlier levels, and these efforts paid off at a G8 meeting in L'Aquila, Italy, in July 2009, when President Barack Obama persuaded rich country leaders to collectively pledge $22 billion for agricultural development over the next three years, of which $6 billion was to be new money. The president leveraged his argument by making a highly personal reference to the impoverished conditions still experienced by his own extended family living in the agricultural countryside in Kenya.

Many donor countries fell short of fulfilling this 2009 pledge. As the three-year period was coming to a close, a respected humanitarian NGO named the One Campaign reported that only about half of the pledged money had been disbursed or firmly committed. Even so, agricultural development assistance spending did increase markedly following the price spike of 2008. In the United States, for example, annual congressional funding for bilateral and multilateral agricultural development assistance increased from $245 million in fiscal year 2008, up to $639 million in fiscal year 2009, and then all the way up to $1.3 billion by fiscal year 2012.

Which agencies operate United States agricultural development assistance?

Most United States assistance programs for agricultural development are planned by officials from USAID working in coordination with individual recipient country governments. They are then implemented by non-governmental organizations from the United States, such as CARE or ACDI/VOCA. The activities funded in this manner include technical support and training for local farmer organizations, support for local seed and fertilizer dealers, and assistance in the marketing and processing of agricultural goods. USAID has significantly increased its own in-house capacity to design agricultural projects since the Obama administration launched a "Feed the Future" initiative in 2010, but most of the work on the ground continues to be outsourced to private contractors.

The other federal government agency that designs and funds significant agricultural development assistance programs is the Millennium Challenge Corporation (MCC), created by the Bush administration in 2004 to provide an alternative to the USAID approach. The MCC operates by making bilateral five-year grants based on detailed "compacts" negotiated with recipient governments, outlining the investments that will be made by the receiving government through its own locally established Millennium Development Authority (MiDA). Congress appropriates the full value of the compact before the agreement is signed, then the funds are disbursed by the MCC in installments. In the agricultural area, the MCC has specialized in funding infrastructure investments, such as an irrigation project in drought-prone Mali and rural road building in northern Ghana. Originally envisioned as a $5-billion-per-year program, the MCC has never been given adequate resources. Congress was not comfortable appropriating foreign assistance money five years in advance, and many Democrats have not been comfortable supporting what is still seen as a Republican innovation in assistance administration.

The United States also supports agricultural development through appropriations for the multilateral International Development Association (IDA) within the World Bank, plus a new Global Agriculture and Food Security Program (GAFSP), a pooled fund also managed by the World Bank. The GAFSP was created following a 2009 G20 Summit meeting, as yet another response to the 2008 food price spike. Unfortunately, international support for GAFSP proved weak, and even the United States faltered in supporting this fund, partly because the 2010 midterm elections put the House of Representatives into the hands of spending-conscious Republicans influenced by the Tea Party movement. In 2012, these same Republicans attacked USAID's assistance programs as well, threatening the durability of President Obama's Feed the Future initiative.

Who benefits from agricultural development assistance?

The beneficiaries include small as well as large farmers. In Ethiopia, for example, USAID supports a Pastoralist Livelihoods

Initiative that organizes women into groups to get credits that they can use either to buy sheep and goats or to diversify into horticulture production, and also a Productive Safety Net Program (PSNP) that funds local community-designed projects to build or repair rural roads, dig wells, plant tree seedlings, or construct school classrooms. United States agricultural development assistance in Ethiopia increased from only $7 million a year in 2007 to $85 million in 2012. By one calculation, the benefits included an additional month of food security for the poor, measured in terms of children's meals consumed during the lean season. When a record drought struck the Horn of Africa in 2011, Ethiopia avoided famine and the number of citizens needing emergency food relief was only half as great as during an earlier drought in 2002–2003.

Increased agricultural development assistance to Bangladesh has also brought tangible benefits. Annual United States assistance to Bangladesh grew from only $6 million in 2009 to $77 million by 2012. These funds made possible a number of initiatives, such as expanded use of a "fertilizer deep placement" technique that allows rice farmers to increase yields by 25 percent while reducing fertilizer use and runoff by 40 percent. The number of rural households benefiting directly from United States agricultural development programs in Bangladesh increased from 119,000 in 2008 to 2,700,000 by 2012.

Despite such demonstrated benefits, political support for agricultural development assistance remains fragile. The 2008 "world food crisis" triggered an overdue revival of resource commitments for these projects, but as the memory of that crisis fades, support for spending in this area could fade as well. In 2012, with Congress threatening cuts to the USAID budget, the Obama administration began looking for a backup approach. It turned to private food and agribusiness companies and launched what it called a New Alliance on Food Security and Nutrition, based on pledges of corporate support for African agriculture. Under this New Alliance, a total of 45 different multinational and African companies committed to make more than $3 billion worth of investments in Africa, spanning every link in the agricultural value chain including irrigation, crop protection, and financing. Substituting private investment for public sector assistance is a worthy long-term goal for Africa, but until adequate public investments are made in rural roads, power, and farming research, the incentives for private firms to do enough will remain weak.

6

THE GREEN REVOLUTION CONTROVERSY

What was the green revolution?

The original green revolution, which took place in the 1960s and 1970s, was an introduction of newly developed wheat and rice seeds into Latin America and into the irrigated farming lands of South Asia and Southeast Asia. These new seed varieties had been developed by plant breeders working in Mexico and the Philippines with support from the non-profit Rockefeller Foundation. The new seeds were capable of producing much higher yields per hectare if grown with adequate applications of water and fertilizer. By cross-breeding different seed varieties from all over the world, the plant scientists had managed to incorporate dwarfing genes which produced short rice and wheat plants that devoted more of their energy to producing grain, and less to straw or leaf material. Short, stiff straws also helped to hold a heavier weight of grain.

Farmers in India began planting the new wheat varieties in 1964, and by 1970 production had nearly doubled. The seeds were introduced not by private companies, but instead by not-for-profit organizations such as the Rockefeller and Ford foundations, with support from donor agencies such as the U.S. Agency for International Development (USAID) plus the government of India itself, which was devoting more than 20 percent of its budget to agricultural development by the early 1970s. Between 1964 and 2008, according to the United Nations Food and Agriculture Organization (FAO), average wheat yields per hectare in India increased fourfold. New rice seeds gave an equally spectacular performance. In India, rice production in the states of Punjab and Haryana doubled between 1971 and 1976. In Asia overall, rice output had been increasing at only a 2.1 percent annual rate during the two decades before the new varieties were introduced in 1965, but output then grew for the next two decades at a much higher 2.9 percent rate. This significant boost in Asia's capacity to produce basic grains arrived at a critical moment when population growth was at its peak, and supporters of the new seeds credit them with saving the region from what would otherwise have been a dangerous food crisis. In 1970, the American scientist who did the most to develop and promote the new wheat varieties, Norman Borlaug, was awarded a Nobel Peace Prize.

Green revolution seed improvements did not end with wheat and rice. Significantly improved varieties of sorghum, millet, barley, and cassava had been developed by the 1980s. Overall, more than 8,000 new seed varieties were introduced for at least 11 different crops. Robert Evenson, an economist at Yale University, calculated in 2003 that if these modern varieties had not been introduced after 1965, annual crop production in the developing world in the year 2000 would have been 16–19 percent lower than it actually was, and world food and feed prices would have been 35–65 percent higher.

Why is the green revolution controversial?

Despite offering dramatic production gains, the new seeds of the green revolution were surrounded by political controversy from the start. Some critics feared that they would lead to greater income inequality if only larger farmers were able to adopt them. Others worried that they would make farmers too dependent on the purchase of expensive inputs such as fertilizer. Still others feared environmental damage from excessive fertilizer applications, excessive pumping of groundwater for irrigation, or the excessive spraying of pesticides. The new seeds were also criticized on the grounds that they could reduce biodiversity if vast monocultures of newly introduced green revolution varieties replaced diverse plantings of traditional crop varieties. At an extreme, some critics even argued that the green revolution seeds had become a source of violent conflict in India, between Hindus and Muslims in the Punjab. In Central America, others blamed green revolution farming for rural dispossession and revolutionary violence.

The response of most farmers to the green revolution was to adopt the new seeds as quickly as possible, as a pathway to increased productivity and higher income. The most vocal critics of the green revolution were not farmers, but instead activists and political leaders who expressed faith in traditional practices, were suspicious of private seed and fertilizer companies, and feared that coaxing higher yields from the land would prove environmentally damaging and unsustainable. The most outspoken green revolution critics, including Indian activist Vandana Shiva, called for farmers to retreat from the modern global marketplace and return to the use of seed varieties based on the "indigenous knowledge" of local farming communities.

These different views toward the original green revolution regularly re-emerge in contemporary political debates about food and farming. Supporters of the original green revolution are eager now to spread the use of improved seeds, fertilizers, and irrigation to regions such as Sub-Saharan Africa. The original green revolution had little impact in Africa, due to a lack of road and water infrastructure and also because wheat and rice were not leading food staples in Africa. To overcome these barriers, the Rockefeller Foundation and the Bill and Melinda Gates Foundation formed a partnership in 2006 called an "Alliance for a Green Revolution in Africa," or AGRA. Green revolution critics responded immediately that such a project would be a serious mistake. Peter Rosset, speaking for a nongovernmental organization in the United States named Food First, warned that the most likely result of this new initiative would be "higher profits for the seed and fertilizer industries, negligible impacts on total food production and a worsening exclusion and marginalization in the countryside."

One explanation for these dramatically divergent views of the green revolution is the differing impact that the new seeds had in Asia versus Latin America. In Asia the benefits of the new seed varieties were widely shared by the poor, while in many parts of Latin America they were not. Today's advocates for the green revolution draw most of their evidence from the positive Asian experience, while critics like to reference the malfunctions they saw in Latin America.

Did the green revolution end hunger?

The green revolution has helped to reduce the prevalence of hunger in Asia today, compared to the hunger we would see if there had been no green revolution. Food became more abundant in the marketplace, and hence less costly for the poor, which enabled an increase in consumption. It also boosted the productivity of farms and hence the incomes of the farmers who adopted the new seeds. In addition, it benefited farmworkers, who found greater employment as harvests grew in size, as well as those who worked in the rural industries that thrived around the transport, storage, and processing of the additional food. These broad-based income gains brought improved nutrition. Studies done at the microlevel during the early years of the green revolution in Asia found that the higher crop yields typically led to greater calorie and protein intake among rural households within adopting regions. For example, economists Per Pinstrup-Andersen and Mauricio Jaramillo, examining the significant dietary improvements seen in one district in southern India in the 1980s, calculated that one-third of the increased calorie intake could be attributed to the increased rice production made possible by the new seeds.

The improved seed technologies of the green revolution also triggered more rapid urban industrial development in Asia. In India, every 1 percent increase in the agricultural growth rate stimulated a 0.5 percent addition to the growth rate of industrial output, boosting incomes and reducing hunger in urban areas. China had a similar experience. When the government of China undertook reforms in 1978 that gave peasant households an incentive to make use of improved seed and fertilizer systems, agricultural production increased over the next two decades at an accelerated 5.1 percent annual rate, according to World Bank calculations, setting a foundation for the rapid urban industrial growth that has now followed. As a result, and despite continued population growth, the number of Chinese people unable to feed, clothe, or adequately house themselves declined from 250 million in 1978 down to only 34 million by 1999, as reported by Chinese economists in 2000 at a development forum in Beijing. Never before had so many people escaped poverty and malnutrition in such a short period of time. The uptake of more productive farm technologies had been key to this success; between 1975 and 1990, according to economists Jikun Huang and Scott Rozelle, the new rice technologies developed independently by Chinese researchers, such as hybrid rice seeds and single-season varieties, made possible over half of the yield increases behind the achievement.

Still, the green revolution by itself did not end hunger in Asia. Overall calorie consumption increased, but in some cases dietary diversity decreased as rice monoculture systems led to diminished consumption of leafy vegetables and fish. Elsewhere, the green revolution did not go far enough. In India, some rural communities were not touched by the green revolution due to inadequate rainfall and no irrigation, or because land tenure systems denied access to the poor. Economic growth rates increased in India overall, most dramatically after the 1990s, but in states such as Gujarat and Rajasthan there has been little improvement in nutrition, particularly regarding micronutrient deficits. As a consequence, India today remains home to roughly 40 percent of all the world's malnourished children. In 2007, Prime Minister Manmohan Singh, in his 60th Anniversary Independence Day Address to the nation, candidly described India's malnutrition problem as "a matter of national shame."

Did the green revolution lead to greater rural inequality?

It did in Latin America, but not in most of Asia. Outcomes differed in these two regions because of some important underlying social differences in the countryside. In much of Latin America, ownership of productive land and access to credit for the purchase of essential green revolution inputs like fertilizer were restricted to a privileged rural elite. When a highly productive new farm technology is introduced into such a system, only the narrow elite will be able to take it up, so inequality will worsen. In most of Asia, by contrast, access to good agricultural land and credit was not so narrowly controlled, which allowed the uptake of the new seeds to be more widely shared, with gains that were far more equitable.

The history of farming in Latin America is one of long-standing social injustice. Indigenous populations went into a tragic decline soon after the arrival of Columbus, falling an estimated 75 percent by 1650 due to a combination of brutal treatment by the Spanish and Portuguese conquerors, plus deadly exposure to unfamiliar European diseases. The Europeans then replaced indigenous farming with vast semi-feudal *hacienda* estates, on which peasants farmed small plots for subsistence purposes without any secure right to land. To the present day, ownership of the best farming land in Latin America remains in the hands of a small commercial elite. Among the rest, some own smaller plots of less productive land, but many own nothing at all. For every 100 smallholder farmers in Latin America who do own some land, 82 others do not.

These severe rural inequalities were in some places worsened by the introduction of green revolution technologies. The commercial farming elite adopted the new seeds quickly, partly because they received government subsidies to help them purchase the fertilizers and pesticides used with the seeds. The elite commercial farmers were also given subsidized credits, research and extension assistance, new irrigation canals for their land, and exemptions from import duties on equipment like farm tractors. Poor farmers were excluded from these government benefits. Agricultural land was made more valuable by the new seeds, but this backfired on many poor farmers who had previously been allowed to plant corn and beans for subsistence on land they did not own. They would now be pushed off by the landlords, to make way for expanded commercial production of high-value crops like cotton. Some of the evicted peasants gained limited compensation in the form of seasonal employment as hired cotton pickers, but otherwise they were forced to shift their farming efforts onto more fragile sloping lands with no access to irrigation and with less fertile soil. Others decided to become slum dwellers on the fringes of the urban economy.

Asia had a different experience with the green revolution seeds, because most farming was dominated not by large estates but by smaller family plots, many with access to irrigation. Because the new seeds were a biological technology, it was not necessary to have a large farm to make use of them (the opposite is true for mechanical technologies, such as tractors). Even tenant farmers who rented land could use the seeds, so long as they had irrigation and could get access to credit. In fact, the International Rice Research Institute found, in one study of 30 rice-growing villages in Asia between 1966 and 1972, that small farms (less than 1 hectare in size) actually adopted the new seeds more quickly than larger farms (over 3 hectares in size). The higher yielding green revolution varieties also brought a substantial increase in annual farm labor demand per unit of cropped land, which pushed up rural wages to the benefit of the landless poor. In some cases, inequality gaps developed between regions that had abundant irrigation and those that did not, but small as well as large growers benefited in places where farmers had water and credit.

The poverty reduction gains that came from the green revolution in Asia were dramatic. The International Food Policy Research Institute calculated that in 1975, early in the history of the green revolution, nearly 60 percent of Asians still lived on $1 a day or less. By 1995, this number had fallen to only 30 percent. Poverty continues to decline in rural Asia, as improved farming technologies have become pervasive.

Farmers large and small show no interest in abandoning the new seeds, yet this does not silence determined critics. In 2002, a forum of NGOs in Rome claimed that green revolution techniques were causing a rise in world hunger. In 2004, a coalition of 670 separate NGOs sent an open letter to the director general of the United Nations FAO warning against the technical fix approach to agricultural development, and referring to the green revolution as a "tragedy."

Was the green revolution bad for the environment?

The environmental impacts of the green revolution also differed in Latin America compared to Asia. In Latin America, two distinct kinds of environmental damage from green revolution farming tended to emerge side by side. On the best lands controlled by politically favored elites, government subsidies induced excessive irrigation, too much fertilizer use, and excessive sprays of chemical pesticides, leading to occupational hazards on the farm plus pollution of the air and water downstream. In Mexico between 1961 and 1989, fertilizer subsidies led to an 800 percent increase in nitrogen fertilizer use per hectare; over the decade of the 1970s, pesticide use increased at an average annual rate of more than 8 percent.

In the Culiacan Valley, subsidized commercial tomato growers began spraying pesticides on their crops as often as 25 to 50 times each growing season.

Meanwhile, a different kind of environmental damage was done by poor farmers in Latin America on non-irrigated land who lacked subsidies and credits and did not participate in the green revolution. These farmers continued using too little fertilizer rather than too much, which exhausted their soils and forced them to move onto even more fragile lands or into forest margins. In Honduras, where the population doubled between 1970 and 1990 and where the poorest two-thirds of all farmers were trapped on just 10 percent of the nation's total farming area, destitute peasants eroded or exhausted their soils and cut much of the remaining forest cover. In Mexico, where half of all farmers were trying to subsist on only 10 percent of the nation's farmland, population growth among the rural poor led to an expanded area under low-yield farming that devastated the environment. In the Mixteca region, according to a 1990 study by environmental scholar Angus Wright, 70 percent of the potentially arable land had lost its ability to grow crops due to soil erosion. Large parts of rural Mexico came to resemble a lifeless moonscape.

Excessive water and pesticide use became a problem in many Asian countries as well, frequently due to unwise government subsidies, just as in Latin America. For example, in Punjab in northwest India in the 1980s, the government rewarded politically powerful commercial farming interests by paying 86 percent of their electric bill for pumping irrigation water. This resulted in excess water use and a precipitous drop in groundwater tables. In Indonesia in the early 1980s, the government subsidized fertilizer purchases by 68 percent, causing fertilizer use to grow by more than two-thirds. This increased nitrates in drinking water and brought nutrient runoff to streams and ponds, resulting in unwanted algae growth. Indonesia also offered an 85 percent subsidy to farmers who purchased pesticides, so excessive spraying on rice fields soon killed the good species, such as spiders, that had earlier helped to keep bad insects under control. The bad insects, such as brown planthoppers, in the meantime evolved to resist the chemical sprays. The government was finally prompted in 1986 to ban the spraying of 57 different insecticides on rice, a move that allowed the natural enemies of the hoppers to recover, eventually bringing the damage under control.

As serious as such green revolution problems were in Asia, the only thing worse might have been to introduce no high-yield seeds at all. If India had been forced to rely on its pre–green revolution, low-yield farming techniques to secure the production gains it needed during these decades of rapid population growth, there would have been no option but to expand the area under cultivation by cutting more trees, destroying more wildlife habitat, and plowing up more fragile sloping or dryland soils. According to M. S. Swaminathan, one of the scientists who led the green revolution in India, the new seeds helped India avoid "a tremendous onslaught on fragile lands and forest margins." In 1964, Swaminathan points out, India produced 12 million tons of wheat on 14 million hectares of land. Thirty years later, thanks to the Green Revolution, India was producing 57 million tons of wheat on 24 million hectares of land. To produce this much wheat using the old seeds would have required roughly 60 million hectares, implying that an additional 36 million hectares would have been put under the plow.

Why did the original green revolution not reach Africa?

Green revolution farming has been slow to reach Sub-Saharan Africa. Between 1970 and 1998, while the share of cropped area planted to modern green revolution varieties increased to 82 percent in the developing regions of Asia, and up to 52 percent in Latin America, only 27 percent of such areas was planted to such varieties in Sub-Saharan Africa. As a consequence, average cereal yields in Africa remained at only 1.1

tons per hectare versus 2.8 tons per hectare in Latin America and 3.7 tons per hectare in Asia. FAO data show that Africa's cereal production per capita actually declined by 5 percent between 1980 and 2000.

Early efforts were made in the 1960s and 1970s to introduce green revolution seed varieties into Africa, but there was little adoption because the international assistance agencies introducing the seeds had tried to jump over the tedious and time-consuming step of using locally adapted plants when breeding for yield improvements. Varieties not suited to African conditions were brought in from Latin America and Asia, and African farmers did not like them. This error was belatedly corrected when more location-specific breeding programs were launched at the beginning of the 1980s, but by then, international assistance for such programs had begun to falter. The success of the green revolution in Asia in the 1960s and 1970s, plus lower international food prices, had convinced many donors that the world food problem had been solved, so they redirected funding away from agriculture just as Africa was finally in a position to benefit.

African farmers were also slow to take up new seed varieties because their lands had a more complex mix of agroecologies, and much of the land was poorly suited to conventional irrigation. Access to farmland in Africa is generally more equitable than in either Latin America or Asia, but only 4 percent of agricultural land in Africa is irrigated. When farmers must rely entirely on uncertain rainfall, the incentive to invest in improved farming technologies weakens, since the investment can be wasted if the rains fail. Africa's weak rural road systems, which cut farmers off from markets, are another problem. Roughly 70 percent of rural Africans live more than 2 kilometers from the nearest all-weather road. Finally, Africa's dominant food crops were not wheat and rice, the lead crops of the green revolution, but instead root crops like sweet potato or cassava, or other legumes and grains such as cowpea, white maize, sorghum, and millet.

More recently, improved farming technologies have begun to find their way into rural Africa, thanks in part to a reduction in violent conflict, advances in democracy, stronger civil societies, the AGRA initiative, and stronger efforts by international donors and national governments under the vision of an African Union Comprehensive Africa Agriculture Development Programme (CAADP) that explicitly targets increased farm productivity. Recent data from the World Bank show that Africa's agricultural GDP growth rate has increased from an average of 2.5 percent per year in the 1990s, which was no more than the rate of growth of population, to an average of 3.1 percent per year in the 2000s, and up to an average of 3.7 percent per year specifically between 2007 and 2010. Significant green revolution productivity gains are now being captured by African maize farmers, and yield growth for root and tuber crops in Africa increased by 40 percent between 1980 and 2005. Rates of poverty and undernutrition in Africa, as noted earlier, have finally started coming down.

What farming approaches do green revolution critics favor?

Critics of the green revolution believe that rural poverty can be reduced and farm productivity enhanced without introducing high-yielding seeds and more chemical fertilizers. These critics prefer farming models based on "agroecology," which is an application of ecological principles to food production. This approach prefers farming systems that imitate nature, rather than those that try to dominate nature. This can mean using crop rotations and manuring rather than chemical fertilizers to replace soil nutrients, or natural biological controls for pests rather than chemical controls, and small diversified farms rather than large specialized farms. Polycultures (a variety of crops in a field) are favored over monocultures, water-harvesting systems rather than large-scale irrigation, and a reliance on local community-based knowledge rather than laboratory science. Many advocates for agroecology start with a view that nature knows best. Human efforts to dominate biological systems will always fail, or trigger unintended consequences.

One early advocate for agroecology as an alternative to the green revolution was Miguel Alteiri, an ecosystem biologist originally from Chile, who looked at farming systems in Latin America in the 1980s, where the green revolution came in for early criticism. Alteiri promoted the enhancement of traditional or indigenous knowledge systems as an alternative to the exotic and reductionist green revolution approach. Alteiri insisted on balancing any search for short-term productivity with an insistence on long-term stability, social equity, and sustainability. Green revolution advocates would contend that their approach can also be stable, equitable, and sustainable, as long as access to land and credit is widely shared, and as long as continuing investments are made in new seed varieties to stay ahead of evolving pest and disease pressures. Agroecology advocates mistrust the technical fix approach, doubting the ability of laboratory science to stay ahead of such pressures forever.

Advocates for agroecology have gained prominent endorsements for their views. For example, an International Assessment of Agricultural Knowledge, Science and Technology for Development (known as the IAASTD) that was completed in 2008 warned that relying on science and technology to increase agricultural productivity—the green revolution approach— would bring too many "unintended social and environmental consequences." This assessment, conducted under the auspices of the World Bank and the United Nations, asserts that the model of innovation that drove the original green revolution "requires revision." It calls for more emphasis on agroecological approaches, organic approaches, and the incorporation of "traditional and local knowledge." The IAASTD assessment was rejected by green revolution supporters, who complained that it had been influenced too heavily by the participation of non-scientists, including technology critics from NGOs such as Greenpeace International, Friends of the Earth International, and the Pesticide Action Network.

Some agroecological approaches, such as introducing biological controls for pests, or agroforestry (the mixing of trees
with crops, or with pasture), have been scaled up with success. More extreme versions, such as those that reject the use
of new seeds or synthetic chemicals, tend to be less productive than conventional green revolution approaches, because
they require more land and more human labor. Advocates for
agroecology deny that there is any disadvantage in their methods and point to a 2008 United Nations study purporting to
show that agroecological and organic systems in developing
countries can register strong yield gains over time, eventually
"matching those in more conventional, input-intensive systems." Critics respond that measures of crop yield per hectare
need to take labor costs into account. Actual farming communities usually prefer labor-saving green revolution approaches
over the labor-intensive agroecological approach.

There is no example, so far, of a country that has made its
farmers prosperous and its people well fed using a strict agroecological approach. The most successful farming systems are
usually those that integrate some agroecological techniques
with green revolution seeds and methods. Crop rotations, such
as planting corn in a field one year and soybeans the next, are
embraced by conventional as well as agroecological farmers.
Pest management techniques that integrate biological controls
with chemical controls are another example. Combining agroecological techniques such as planting leguminous trees alongside a field of high-yield hybrid maize, then using a judicious
amount of chemical fertilizer, is another integrated strategy.

The most rapidly growing system for integrating agroecology with conventional farming is called "no-till" farming,
in which farmers do not plow the ground before planting.
Instead, they use specialized machinery to sow seeds directly
through crop residues from the previous harvest. This method
retains soil moisture, protects the soil against erosion from
runoff, and saves time and money by eliminating plowing.
Conventional farmers in the United States started moving

toward this method in the 1970s, as a response to high fuel costs, and now the technique has spread to many other countries as well. Currently, about 75 percent of Brazil's cropland is managed without tillage.

Many advocates for agroecology are uncomfortable with no-till farming on a commercial scale because it requires specialized machinery that small farmers with diversified cropping systems cannot afford, and because controlling weeds without tillage often means using herbicides, or even genetically engineered seeds. Nevertheless, it is a proven method in both poor and rich countries for conserving soil and water while boosting crop yields. In 2012, IFPRI reported that on the Indo-Gangetic Plains, Indian farmers using reduced tillage practices spent an average of $55 per hectare less in cultivation costs, saved 50–60 liters of fuel and 15–50 percent of water, and increased their crop yields by 247 kilograms per hectare. Methods such as these can help put the green revolution on a more sustainable path.

How have green revolution critics shaped international policy?

The political controversy over green revolution farming versus agroecology continues to rage among international policy makers, particularly within the United Nations system, where environmental and social justice NGOs have gained a strong voice. These NGOs have fought to promote agroecological and organic approaches to farming, in place of green revolution methods that rely on purchased inputs and modern agricultural science. This advocacy had an impact on the foreign assistance policies of donor countries beginning in the 1980s; international assistance was reduced for new irrigation projects in the developing world, new seed development, and sales of chemical fertilizers.

Between 1980 and 2003, the real dollar value of all bilateral assistance to help modernize agriculture in the developing world declined by 64 percent, from $5.3 billion (in constant

1999 U.S. dollars) to just $1.9 billion. United States assistance to new agricultural research in Africa declined by 77 percent. This withdrawal of donor support had little effect in Latin America and Asia, where agricultural modernization had already taken off and became self-sustaining, but it left the aid-dependent governments in Africa without enough external support to begin a confident move of their own down the green revolution path.

Criticism of the green revolution became particularly strong in the environmental community. In 1992 Senator Al Gore, soon to become vice president, published a best-selling book titled *Earth in the Balance* that depicted the green revolution as a dangerous Faustian bargain, one that used environmentally unsustainable techniques to secure yield gains that would be only temporary. Yet FAO data reveal that in the two decades after Gore issued this warning, global cereal yields continued to increase annually at the same constant linear rate (43 kilograms per hectare) that had prevailed in the two decades before Gore wrote. Later in the 1990s, advocates for modern agricultural science, such as Gordon Conway, called for new research investments in a "doubly green revolution" designed to increase yields while at the same time protecting the environment and ensuring benefits for the poor, but agroecology advocates were not attracted to this compromise because it seemed to include investments in genetically engineered crops.

Even with revived concerns about the world food supply following the international food price spike of 2007–2008, the green revolution approach remained under a political cloud. The new concerns led to greater donor assistance for agricultural development, particularly in Africa, but always against a background warning from critics—in reports such as the IAASTD—that the green revolution path would sooner or later prove unsustainable. Green revolution critics even argued that the higher international food prices were, in some way, proof that the gains from current methods had been exhausted. Actual measures of total factor productivity growth in conventional agriculture did not support this view. A 2008 study by economist Keith Fuglie in the journal *Agricultural Economics* revealed that, among the developing countries as a whole, the growth rate of total factor productivity in agriculture had been twice as high in the 1991–2006 period as during the earlier 1970–1990 period.

The green revolution continues to be criticized by most organized environmentalists and social justice advocates in rich countries, yet it remains the approach of choice among most farmers and agricultural policy leaders in the developing world. In China and India today, green revolution seed varieties grown in monocultures with nitrogen fertilizer have become the pervasive means of food production and continue to be strongly promoted by the state. In fact, both China and India have now moved beyond the original green revolution method of seed improvement to embrace, for at least some crops, a more recent science-based approach: genetically engineered seeds (to be discussed in Chapter 13).

7

THE POLITICS OF OBESITY

Is the world facing an obesity crisis?

Worldwide, obesity rates have nearly doubled in the last three decades. In 1980, 5 percent of men and 8 percent of women around the world were obese. By 2008, the rates were 10 percent for men and 14 percent for women. The problem is currently concentrated in North America and parts of Europe. In the United States, as of 2010, 36 percent of adults were obese. In England and Ireland in 2007, the rates of adult obesity were 25 percent and 22 percent, respectively. The UN World Health Organization (WHO) projects that in 2015 there will be a total of 2.3 billion overweight adults worldwide, 700 million of whom will be technically obese. In other words, there will be nearly as many obese people on earth as there are undernourished people. The problem of hunger that previously monopolized political attention is now sharing the stage with this new and rapidly growing problem of excessive food consumption.

How do we measure obesity?

Obesity is a crude measure of the roundness of the body, based on a body mass index (BMI), which is body weight (in kilograms), divided by the square of height (in meters). People with a BMI between 25 and 30 are considered overweight; those with a BMI above 30 are obese; and those with a BMI above 40 are described as severely obese. Translating to more familiar terms, a 6-foot-tall individual is considered overweight above 183 pounds, obese above 220 pounds, and severely obese above 295 pounds. Adverse health consequences become far more likely as individuals go from merely overweight to obese. Those in the United States who are moderately obese have personal health care costs 20–30 percent higher than those with a healthy weight, and severe obesity more than doubles health care costs. Some studies show that obesity, on average, reduces life expectancy by 6 to 7 years.

Between 1971 and 2010 in the United States, the prevalence of obesity among adults more than doubled from 14.5 percent to 36 percent. Between 2000 and 2010 alone, the rate of severe obesity among adults increased from 3.9 percent to 6.6 percent. In other words, roughly 15 million adult Americans are now 100 pounds or more over what is considered a healthy weight. Among children in the United States, the rate of obesity has increased even more dramatically, from 5 percent in 1980 up to 17 percent today. In 2012, the Robert Wood Johnson Foundation projected that if obesity rates continue on their current trajectories, 39 states will have rates above 50 percent by 2030, and all 50 states will have rates above 44 percent.

America remains in the lead on obesity, but other countries are now following a parallel path. In Canada today, 19.5 percent of boys under the age of 18 are obese. In Brazil since the 1980s, rates of obesity among children have increased from 4 percent up to 14 percent. Even in Japan, which has the lowest adult obesity rate in the developed world (just 3.9 percent), childhood obesity is on the rise. In Japan between 1980 and 2000, the prevalence of obesity among 10-year-old boys increased from 6 percent to 11 percent.

What are the consequences of the obesity epidemic?

Strictly speaking, obesity is not a medical condition. It is perfectly possible for individuals to be both heavy and healthy.

Yet within larger populations, as obesity rates increase, the probability that individuals will develop ailments such as type 2 diabetes, high blood pressure, and high blood cholesterol will increase as well. The link between body shape and health can be challenged: one 2013 study concluded that increased sugar consumption was the key link to diabetes, independent of obesity. In 2012, however, the Centers for Disease Control (CDC) reported that between 1995 and 2010, the prevalence of diagnosed diabetes had increased by 50 percent or more in 42 states, and by 100 percent in more than 18 states. "These rates will continue to increase until effective interventions and policies are implemented to prevent both diabetes and obesity," said the CDC.

Organizations that campaign against obesity paint a dark picture of the future. According to one projection from the Robert Wood Johnson Foundation, if the current trajectory of obesity continues in the United States between 2010 and 2020, the number of new cases of type 2 diabetes, coronary heart disease, stroke, hypertension, and arthritis could increase 10 times. By 2030, obesity could contribute to more than 6 million cases of type 2 diabetes, 5 million cases of coronary heart disease and stroke, and more than 400,000 cases of cancer. By 2050, life expectancy in the United States may be shortened by 2 to 5 years.

Obesity is primarily a personal and family concern, but compounding medical costs make it a public health issue as well. In the United States between 1998 and 2008, the medical costs of treating obesity-related diseases doubled to reach $147 billion, about 9 percent of all medical costs. By 2030, if trends continue unchecked, obesity-related medical costs could rise by another $48–66 billion a year in the United States.

The heaviest costs of obesity can be personal, in the form of reduced employment and income options, social isolation, and depression. Days missed from work, more frequent hospitalizations, and more expensive medical insurance all have social as well as personal impacts. Obesity is even a national security issue. In 2010, a panel of retired military officers found that 27 percent of all young adults in America were "too fat to serve in the military." Between 1995 and 2008, the percentage of potential recruits who failed their physicals due to being overweight increased by nearly 70 percent.

What is the cause of today's obesity epidemic?

Obesity results when the human body persistently takes in, through eating and drinking, more caloric energy than it burns through basic metabolism and muscular exertion. The modern obesity epidemic derives from both an increase in average caloric intake and a decrease in average muscular exertion. Genetic inheritance helps explain some of the occurrence of obesity person by person within generations, but it cannot explain the rapid increase that we have seen in prevalence across generations, because human genetics does not change that fast.

Increased calorie intake is the single largest source of the problem. In the United States between 1970 and 2003, average daily caloric intake increased 23 percent to a level of 2,757 calories, which is roughly 20 percent more than the World Health Organization recommends. Among children in America between 1977 and 2006, average calorie consumption increased 10 percent. Meanwhile, average muscular exertion declined, as travel took place less often on foot and more often by car, and as physical demands in both the home and the workplace were reduced. Most work in America now takes place while sitting in chairs, or behind the wheel of a vehicle. In the home, rugs, dishes, and clothing are now cleaned with electrical power rather than muscular exertion. The removal of snow, the cutting of grass, and the trimming of hedges have all been motorized. Washing automobiles is now automated, and seasonal chores such as hanging storm windows no longer exist. Stair climbing has been replaced by elevators. Only 4 percent of elementary schools, 8 percent of middle schools, and 2 percent of high schools now provide daily physical education for all students. While 20 percent of trips between school and home were on foot in 1977, that figure had fallen to just 12 percent by 2001. Despite a booming fitness industry, working out has actually declined, as commuting times have lengthened and as more leisure time is now spent sitting in front of the home computer. Among American men 40 to 74 years of age, since 1990 the number of people who report exercising three times a week has dropped from 57 percent to 43 percent. Young people own fancier bicycles but ride them less often. By the late 1990s, the majority of American children watched more than 5 hours of television a day.

Does cheap food cause obesity?

Personal calorie consumption has increased in part because food has become cheap, especially relative to income. Over the course of the twentieth century, the real cost of food commodities declined by 50 percent in the United States, thanks primarily to productivity growth on the farm, while average consumer income was at the same time increasing by roughly 400 percent. Food today is so cheap relative to income that increasing quantities are wasted and often simply thrown away.

The low cost of food in America is sometimes blamed on farm subsidies, but most agricultural economists disagree. One study by three economists published in the journal *Food Policy* in 2008 found that if national farm subsidy policies were eliminated the cost to consumers of soybeans, rice, sugar, fruits and vegetables, beef, pork, and milk would actually fall more, not increase. A later study published in *Health Economics* in 2012 showed that if all farm subsidies were removed—including the measures that reduce imports of cheap food from abroad—the cost to Americans of sugar and dairy products would go down enough to induce a small increase in calorie consumption of about 3,000 to 3,900 additional calories a year for a typical adult.

Critics often assert that farm subsidies in the United States have generated too much corn production, which in turn lowers the price of livestock feed, making meat products artificially cheap. Corn prices have been slightly lowered by some farm policies in recent years, but on balance corn prices have been artificially raised, thanks to other government policies that promote the use of corn for ethanol production. The price of corn has also been driven up by import restrictions on sugar that encourage the use of corn-based sweeteners, such as high fructose corn syrup (HFCS). If sugar import restrictions were removed, the price of both sugar and HFCS in the United States would fall by roughly 15 percent, making sodas, candy, and ice cream even cheaper, and the obesity crisis even worse.

Farm support policies throughout the industrial world actually tend to make food artificially expensive, not artificially cheap, because they so frequently include restrictions on imports. This is even more the case for Europe and Japan than for the United States. According to calculations by the Organisation for Economic Co-operation and Development (OECD), government policies in the European Union in 2009 made food costs for consumers 7 percent higher than they would have been without subsidies, and in Japan 42 percent higher.

Another charge, that junk-food prices have fallen in the United States while fruit and vegetable prices have not, is also questionable. A 2008 study by the Economic Research Service at the U.S. Department of Agriculture (USDA) showed that over the previous 25 years the price of fruit and vegetable products in the marketplace (controlling for quality and season of the year) fell at almost exactly the same rate as the price of chocolate chip cookies, cola, ice cream, and potato chips. Not only are fresh fruits and vegetables cheaper than ever before when sold in season, they are also more widely available out of season. American supermarkets today carry as many as 400 different produce items, up from an average of just 150 different items in the 1970s. Access to healthy and affordable food has been increasing, not decreasing. Unfortunately, access to unhealthy food has increased even more.

Do fast foods and junk foods cause obesity?

Yes, but other foods are a problem as well. In 2011 the *New England Journal of Medicine* published a study that revealed that the top contributors to weight gain in the United States included red meat and processed meats, sugar-sweetened beverages, and potatoes, including mashed potatoes and french fries. The single biggest weight-inducing food was the potato chip. Other studies suggest that the single largest driver of the obesity epidemic is sweetened beverages. The average American today gets more than 450 calories a day from beverages, including juices, dairy drinks, sweetened soft drinks, and alcohol. Beverages provide twice as many calories today as they did in 1965, with more than two-thirds of the increase coming from sweetened fruit juices and soft drinks. Specialists calculate that the recent increase in obesity can be accounted for by the consumption of a single extra 20-ounce soft drink each day. In one study of overweight or obese high schoolers, when the sugary drinks normally consumed were replaced with sugar-free alternatives, average weight loss over a 12-month period was 4 pounds.

It is sometimes alleged that the sweetening of beverages with high fructose corn syrup rather than natural sugar has made those drinks more obesity inducing, but the evidence to support this charge is weak. The HFCS used in soft drinks consists of 55 percent fructose and 45 percent glucose, not significantly different from ordinary sugar, which is 50 percent fructose and 50 percent glucose. Michael Jacobson, director of the Center for Science and the Public Interest, has said that the popular idea that HFCS carries a greater obesity risk is "an urban myth."

Fast food restaurant meals are often an invitation to obesity. It is not unusual for an individual meal to contain more than 1,000 calories. It takes an hour and 20 minutes of jogging to burn off this much energy. A 2013 study from the Center for Science and the Public Interest found that 91 percent of kids' meals at fast food chains in the United States did not even meet the industry's own "Kids LiveWell" nutrition standards. Careful studies that control for variables such as income, education, and race have shown that obesity rates among ninth-grade schoolchildren are 5 percent higher if the school is located within one-tenth of a mile of a fast food outlet. The National Restaurant Association rejects such studies as "slapdash," yet local political pressures are rising to zone fast food restaurants away from public schools, and the fast food chains themselves have responded with visible menu changes. In 2009, Burger King announced three new kids' meals that included smaller burgers, sliced apples designed to look like french fries, reduced-sodium chicken tenders, and fat-free chocolate milk. McDonald's began to offer apples and yogurt.

Is the food industry to blame for the way we eat?

Yes, to an extent. The modern food industry does more than simply process, package, and deliver foods to consumers. It also designs the taste and consistency of those foods, manipulating the ingredients, including the sugar, fat, and salt content, to make them more difficult for consumers to resist. Between 1994 and 2006, food companies in the United States introduced about 600 new children's food products; half were candies or chewing gums, and another one-fourth were other types of sweets or salty snacks. Dr. David Kessler, a former head of the U.S. Food and Drug Administration (FDA), charged in 2009 that modern food companies are in part to blame for our overeating because they design foods for irresistibility, delivering tastes and textures that hit an intentionally addictive "bliss point."

The food industry also advertises foods to children not old enough to understand the health implications of consuming high-calorie, low-nutrient junk foods. American children spend about $30 billion of their own money every year on such foods, and in 2006 an Institute of Medicine study concluded that the choices made were to some extent shaped by corporate marketing. The Center for Science and the Public Interest asserts that the food and beverage industry spends $2 billion every year advertising food to children. Kids aged 2–11 years see an average of 13 food ads a day.

Food companies have now gone beyond television ads, targeting children who use smartphones and laptops as well (in the United States, the average first use of a smartphone takes place at age 7). A favorite vehicle has become online games, available on sites like Candystand.com, pioneered by Kraft Foods and the Wm. Wrigley Jr. Company. Kraft recently released an iPad app, "Dinner, Not Art," in which players slide pieces of Mac & Cheese around the screen to create macaroni art. The United States does less to regulate food advertising than most other wealthy countries. In 1980, Congress barred the Federal Trade Commission from making broad new rules on food advertising to children. Under pressure, some companies have at least taken voluntary action. In 2012, the Walt Disney Company announced that it would no longer accept advertisements for junk food on its child-oriented television and radio sites. Governments in Sweden, Norway, Austria, Luxembourg, Belgium, and Quebec have all banned television junk-food advertising during children's programming.

As calorie consumption has increased overall, the consumption of many nutritious foods in America has actually declined. In 2012, the Department of Agriculture reported that the share of family food budgets going toward the purchase of fruits and vegetables declined between 1998 and 2006. Over the past two decades, the share of Americans aged 40 to 74 who eat five servings of fruits and vegetables a day has dropped from 42 percent to 26 percent. Multiple factors have driven this outcome, including more women working outside of the home (resulting in fewer home-prepared meals), more commuting by car and a rapidly growing preference for meals that can be held in one hand while driving, greater leisure time spent snacking while watching television, and also less cigarette smoking (an appetite suppressant).

The food industry, represented politically in the United States by the Grocery Manufacturers Association (GMA), attempts to present itself as a guardian of consumer health and well-being, "committed to helping arrest and reverse the growth of obesity around the world." The GMA's favored response to the obesity crisis is "consumer education," rather than new taxes or regulations. The Center for Consumer Freedom, an organization funded by restaurant and food industries, warns against taxes and regulations, so as not to "reduce the number of choices Americans have when they sit down to eat."

Just the same, food companies have recently begun to change their behavior even without direct regulation. In 2005, the U.S. Department of Health and Human Services jointly with the Department of Agriculture published new Dietary Guidelines for Americans, which recommended that half of daily grain intake should come from whole grains. In response, bread companies voluntarily reformulated products so they could claim a higher whole grain content (yet some then defeated the purpose by making the reformulation more palatable with added quantities of sugar, salt, or fat). In 2006, the Food and Drug Administration began to require disclosure of trans fat content on food labels, and New York City banned trans fats in restaurant foods. This experience induced a number of food manufacturers, including Nestlé, Kraft, Campbell's, Kellogg's, and Frito-Lay, to reformulate products to eliminate trans fats entirely, and several major food service companies, including McDonald's and Burger King, announced their intent to begin using frying oils with no trans fats. Kentucky Fried Chicken began replacing trans fats before they had to, in anticipation of the New York City ban.

A leading supermarket operator in the United States, Delhaize America, recently began promoting a system called

Guiding Stars, which rates the nutritional value of most of the food and beverage products sold in their stores. Foods that have more vitamins, minerals, dietary fiber, and whole grains, and less fat, sugar, sodium, or cholesterol are given stars. Customer purchases in these supermarkets have shifted significantly toward the products that have been awarded stars. Yet the political power of the food industry has blocked any move to make such a system mandatory.

Do "food deserts" cause obesity?

Obesity is a growing problem among all categories of Americans. Between 1994 and 2008, according to the Centers for Disease Control and Prevention, the prevalence of obesity increased in adults at all income and education levels. Yet factors such as residency, income, education, and race do make a difference. Some of the highest obesity rates are found among African Americans and Hispanics, many of whom live at lower income levels in urban areas. This has given rise to the idea that some modern city dwellers live in "food deserts," where there is a shortage of supermarkets selling fresh fruits and vegetables. Residents may have no choice but to eat at fast food restaurants, or to purchase energy-dense packaged and processed foods from corner convenience stores. When the USDA examined this idea using data from the 2010 census, it found that almost 10 percent of the U.S. population, or roughly 30 million Americans, did live in low-income areas more than 1 mile from a supermarket. However, only 1.8 percent of all households lived more than 1 mile from a supermarket and did not have a vehicle.

Statistically, a convincing link between limited access to supermarkets and obesity has been difficult to establish. Research suggests that the most powerful link may not be low access to supermarkets, but high access to fast food and corner stores. One 2012 study found that poor neighborhoods had nearly twice as many fast food restaurants and convenience stores as wealthier ones. Some low-income Americans also face time burdens that get in the way of preparing nutritious family meals. Single working parents, for example, may be short of time as well as money. At the end of a work day, they find it more convenient to pick up a bucket of KFC fried chicken, instead of shopping at a market, taking the time to prepare a healthy meal at home, and then cleaning up the pots and pans.

Increasingly, our meals are not taken at home. In the United States, away-from-home food spending increased from 26 percent of total food outlays per person in 1970 to 46 percent by 2002. The total number of food service establishments in the country nearly doubled over this same period. Most restaurant menus are geared to pleasure and convenience rather than health. It is revealing that 17 percent of all meals ordered from restaurants in America are now eaten in cars.

Unstructured eating of this kind is no longer unique to the United States. Throughout Europe, a rapid increase in the number of women in the workforce has also undercut traditional at-home meal preparation, creating a parallel shift toward the consumption of high-calorie fast foods and convenience foods. In the United Kingdom, 27 percent of all food spending is now for meals from outside the home, and in Spain, 26 percent. In France, time spent on meal preparation at home has fallen by half since the 1960s, and fast food restaurants are on the rise even in Greece and Portugal. The much-praised Mediterranean diet (based on vegetables, fruit, unrefined grains, and olive oil) is now disappearing even from Mediterranean countries. As fast food chains spread in Greece between 1982 and 2002, the percentage of overweight boys increased by more than 200 percent, and the increase has continued since then. Italy and Spain are not far behind, with more than 50 percent of adults now either overweight or obese. In 2008, the United Nations Food and Agriculture Organization (FAO) issued a report showing that the Mediterranean diet had "decayed into a moribund state."

What government actions are being taken to reverse the obesity crisis?

In the United States, government action at the federal level to combat obesity has so far been weak, while the strongest actions have been taken at the local or municipal level. Stronger national policies have been set in place in Asia and Europe. The strongest policies can be found in the countries where obesity problems are least advanced.

Policy action to combat obesity has been hard for the United States in part because many do not yet see it as a collective problem. One reason is that health care costs in America have not traditionally been socialized; they have been covered instead through employer-provided or private health insurance systems. Many in America claim not to see obesity as a problem at all. Close to half of all obese Americans say that their own body weight is not an issue, and more than 40 percent of parents with obese children describe their child as being "about the right weight." Social acceptance of obesity is actively promoted by civil rights advocates for the overweight, led in the United States by the National Association to Advance Fat Acceptance (NAAFA), an organization that has been operating since 1969.

Governments have a wide array of policy options to consider in response to obesity. At the least coercive end of the spectrum, they can try public education campaigns about healthy eating, or require health ratings on packaged foods, or require calorie counts on restaurant meals. More coercive steps might include restrictions on advertising of some foods to children, or mandatory counseling by primary care physicians. Subsidy policies might be used to reduce the price or increase the availability of nutritious foods, and tax or regulatory policies might be used to increase the price and reduce the availability of energy-dense, non-nutritious foods. On the physical activity side, governments could move back to requiring physical education in schools, or invest more in playgrounds, bike paths, and sidewalks. Mandates, taxes, and regulations are normally the strongest policy instruments available to governments, yet a 2010 study by the OECD revealed that governments in wealthy democratic societies were primarily relying on weak instruments like information campaigns, or on subsidies, to promote more healthful eating choices.

Some governments in Europe and Asia have experimented with stronger measures. In October 2011, Denmark implemented a nationwide 9 percent tax on saturated fat in foods such as bacon, cheese, and butter. Denmark was following Hungary, which had passed a similar tax aimed at products with high sugar, fat, and salt contents (with the revenue going toward health care costs). The Danish tax proved unpopular and was rescinded one year later when it was noted that butter consumption had failed to decline, and when Danes began avoiding the tax by purchasing cheese from across the border in Germany. This discouraging experience gave pause to several other European countries—including Switzerland, the United Kingdom, and Germany—that were considering a similar tax. In France since 2004, the government has been operating a Let's Prevent Obesity in Children program in which children from 5 to 12 years old are weighed and their BMI calculated annually, with a letter to their parents reporting and explaining the result.

The strongest measures so far in the industrial world have been taken by the country with the lowest obesity prevalence, Japan. In 2008, Japan's Ministry of Health adopted a "metabo law" that established waistline standards to be monitored by employers once a year, under Japan's national health care coverage system. If companies did not reduce the number of overweight employees by 10 percent by 2012, and 25 percent by 2015, they would be required to pay more money into a health care program for the elderly. An estimated 56 million Japanese will have their waists measured under this program each year. Even more intrusive was a policy adopted by the non-democratic country of Singapore, which cut down on lunch sizes and kept children after school for mandatory exercise if they failed to control their weight. Obesity prevalence did decline.

In the United States, strong policy measures at the federal level have so far been impossible, thanks in part to the lobbying power of the food and beverage industry. In 2009, when anti-obesity advocates proposed a small tax on the sale of sweetened soft drinks to help pay for national health care reform, the American Beverage Association (ABA), which represents the beverage industry, spent $18.9 million in a lobbying effort that blocked the tax. The beverage industry campaigns hard against soda taxes at the state and local level as well. In 2010, after the state legislature in Washington imposed a small tax on soft drinks to help balance the state budget during the economic recession, the ABA spent $16.5 million to promote a ballot initiative that promptly overturned the tax. In 2012, voters in two midsized California towns rejected soda taxes after the ABA spent several million dollars on advertisements and on paid canvassers to block these measures.

The strongest national legislation currently in place against obesity in the United States is the 2010 Healthy, Hunger-Free Kids Act. This law reformed the National School Lunch Program, which provides meals to 31 million children a day. The new 2010 law expanded the number of low-income children eligible for meal subsidies, so long as schools served increased portions of fruits, vegetables, and whole grains, while limiting sodium, fat, and calories. Advocates for regulating school menus point to a 2007 initiative in Mississippi that led to a 13 percent decline in obesity among elementary school children. Critics observe that students consume only about 25 percent of their calories in school, making this a weak policy instrument.

In addition, the 2010 law was blunted when the frozen pizza industry secured language from Congress qualifying pizza (with tomato sauce) as a vegetable. Potato farmers also managed to block curbs on how often french fries could be served. The responses of schoolchildren to the 2010 law have been mixed. Vegetable servings often end up in the trash. Students in one Pittsburgh suburb organized a lunch strike, and in some other schools participation in the lunch program has fallen by 70 percent. Anticipating that some children might spurn the more nutritious offerings in the cafeteria line and turn instead to candy, chips, or beverages from vending machines, the authors of the law simultaneously empowered the USDA to set national nutrition standards for school vending machine foods and drinks.

A second federal initiative has been First Lady Michelle Obama's 2009 "Let's Move" campaign to reduce childhood obesity. In addition to public education, this campaign sought to persuade Wal-Mart, Walgreens, Supervalu, and other grocers to commit to locating more stores in low-income neighborhoods. In one response, a team of grocery industry groups, health care organizations, and banks commited $200 million to eliminating "food deserts" in California. Also in support of the initiative, Wal-Mart announced that, by 2015, it would remove all trans fats from its stores and reduce salt and added sugars by 25 percent and 10 percent, respectively. Additionally, a restaurant company that owns Olive Garden and Red Lobster committed to reducing total calories and salt across its menus.

By far the strongest government actions to combat obesity in the United States have come at the state and local level. Currently, from 500 to 600 school districts across the country have policies that limit the amount of fat, trans fat, sodium, and sugar in food sold or served at school. The state of California has banned the sale of soft drinks in public schools and since 2007 has specified that snacks sold during the school day must contain no more than 35 percent sugar by weight and derive no more than 35 percent of their calories from fat. In 2012, researchers determined that these measures had helped to reduce high school student food intake in California by 158 calories a day, compared to other states. Vigorous responses at the state and municipal level can make a difference. In New York City and Philadelphia, the number of obese schoolchildren declined by 5 percent between 2007 and 2011, and in Los Angeles by 3 percent.

At the municipal level in the United States, the City of New York has attempted the strongest measures of all, but not always with success. Beginning in 2008 in New York, restaurant chains were obliged to post calorie counts for the dishes they serve; however, one New York University study found that total calories purchased did not change as a result. In 2010, New York City sought permission from the U.S. Department of Agriculture to eliminate caloric soda from eligibility for local purchase under the SNAP program, but this request was refused. In 2012, the city moved to block sales of soda and other high-calorie drinks in containers larger than 16 ounces, but early in 2013, this measure was blocked by a state judge one day before it was set to take effect.

Who lobbies for and against stronger policies on obesity?

In the United States, the most visible advocates for stronger policies on obesity include public interest lobby groups such as the Center for Science and the Public Interest (CSPI), private foundations dedicated to improving health such as the Robert Woods Johnson Foundation, and university-based think tanks such as the Rudd Center for Food Policy and Obesity at Yale University. Individuals who are obese and citizen groups with members who suffer from obesity are not usually in the lead. Those who suffer from obesity more often organize for social acceptance or for the purpose of seeking more affordable treatments. Taxes on sodas or energy-dense snack foods are seen as regressive on the poor and are unpopular even within low-income or minority communities where obesity is a serious problem. For example, the president of the National Association for the Advancement of Colored People (NAACP) openly opposed Mayor Michael R. Bloomberg's 2012 move to ban large servings of sugary drinks. In 2010 when New York asked for permission to exempt soda from SNAP coverage, leaders from the minority community criticized the move as suggesting that SNAP recipients were unable to make smart food choices. A 2013 survey from the Associated Press and the Center for Public Affairs Research revealed that 70 percent of Americans support requirements to post calorie counts on menus, and 80 percent would support requiring more physical activity in school, but 60 percent are opposed to taxes that target unhealthy foods. Only one-third consider obesity a community problem; most consider it to be an issue primarily for individuals.

The strongest opposition to more effective obesity policies in the United States comes from the food and beverage industry, which argues that what we decide to eat should be a personal choice. Kevin Keane, a spokesperson for the American Beverage Association, said in 2009, "It's overreaching when government uses the tax code to tell people what they can eat or drink." When the City of New York attempted to restrict the sale of large drinks in 2012, it was sued by the American Beverage Association, the National Restaurant Association, a soft drink workers union, and groups representing interests ranging from movie theater owners to Korean American grocers. Nationally, a Center for Consumer Freedom, funded by the restaurant and food industry, regularly criticizes any government effort to shape or reduce food choices.

Weak obesity-prevention policies in the United States also derive, to some extent, from the social influence of groups organized not for obesity prevention but for treatment, such as the annual $50 billion diet and exercise industry. Pharmaceutical and medical companies also profit from selling treatments (not cures) for those who develop type 2 diabetes, high blood pressure, and high cholesterol. In contrast, many employers and insurers have a greater interest in prevention than in treatment. The United Health Group now offers a health insurance plan in which a $5,000 yearly deductible can be reduced to $1,000 if a person is not obese and does not smoke. Financial inducements have even been tried. In 2009, the National

Health Service in the United Kingdom ran a pilot program that offered cash payments of up to 425 pounds depending on how much weight was lost (the program was called "pounds for pounds"). Nearly 800 people joined the scheme, but most dropped out. Those who completed the program lost weight, but many subsequently gained it back.

From a public policy perspective, governments must take care not to treat excessive calorie consumption as parallel to cigarette smoking, alcohol abuse, or narcotic drug use. Unlike tobacco, alcohol, or narcotics, calories from food are absolutely essential to human health. And unlike smoking, being obese presents no "passive" health risk to others. Social risks such as impaired driving, domestic violence, and criminal behavior are also missing in the case of obesity. Most important, a significant share of obese people are quite healthy, and for some individuals the condition is driven more by genetics than lifestyle. Government policies that punish or stigmatize such individuals must be avoided. The best intervention is usually private counseling from a trusted personal physician.

8

THE POLITICS OF FARM SUBSIDIES AND TRADE

Do all governments give subsidies to farmers?

Nearly all governments in rich countries subsidize the income of farmers. In 2011, according to calculations by the Organisation for Economic Co-operation and Development (OECD), government policies in 34 rich countries transferred a total of $252 billion worth of income to farmers, mostly by taking it away from taxpayers and food consumers. On average, 19 percent of total farm receipts in these countries came from such government policies, although in some it was much higher (more than 50 percent in Norway, Switzerland, and Japan) and in others much lower (less than 5 percent in Australia, Chile, and New Zealand). In the United States, 8 percent of farm receipts depended on government interventions in 2011, while in the European Union it was 22 percent.

The policies that transfer this income to farmers include direct cash payments, market or trade restrictions to boost crop prices, subsidies to cheapen the purchase of crop insurance, and subsidies intended to reinforce environmentally sustainable planting practices. In the United States, most income transfers to farmers come at the expense of taxpayers, but in countries that support farm income primarily through import restrictions—such as Japan, Korea, Norway, and Switzerland—most of the transfer comes at the expense of consumers, who are being forced to pay much higher prices for food. It is sometimes presumed that farm subsidies make food cheap for consumers by boosting production, but this is not the case. The purpose of farm subsidies is to boost the income of farmers, not to boost food production. Import restrictions do sometimes encourage more domestic crop production, but not enough to make up for the blocked imports, so the prices that domestic food consumers pay are still artificially high, not artificially low.

Governments in poor developing countries provide much less income support to farmers, even though these countries have many more farmers. In fact, poor countries often tax their farmers, while subsidizing food costs for urban consumers. They rig their internal markets to oblige farmers to sell food at an artificially low price, thus creating an income transfer away from farmers and toward food consumers. So while policies in rich countries tend to be rural-biased, policies in many poor countries tend to be urban-biased.

What explains the tendency of all rich countries to subsidize farm income?

Governments usually start subsidizing farmers during the initial stages of their industrial development. All economic sectors gain income and wealth during this industrialization process, including the agricultural sector, but larger farms will start to buy up smaller farms, since a bigger size makes it easier to take advantage of powered machinery such as tractors and harvesting combines. The mechanization process leads to farm consolidation and an out-migration of labor from rural communities. Rural towns will begin to depopulate, small shops will struggle, and public schools will have to consolidate or close. Confronting such changes, smaller farmers will usually organize to seek assistance or protection from government. Feeling that they are losing out in the economic marketplace, they will support lobby group actions in the political market-place that demand income support through tax breaks, subsidized loans, import restrictions, market interventions to raise crop prices, and even direct cash payments.

The countries of Europe were the first to industrialize, so they were also the first to provide subsidy programs of this kind to support farmers, initially during and then after World War I. The United States began regulating agricultural markets and providing subsidy benefits to farmers a bit later, during the Great Depression of the 1930s, through the Agricultural Adjustment Act (AAA) of 1933, as part of President Franklin D. Roosevelt's New Deal program. Japan embraced agricultural subsidy policies still later, when that nation moved toward full industrial development in the 1950s and 1960s; in Taiwan and South Korea, subsidies came still later, when rapid industrial growth reached those countries in the 1970s and 1980s.

The predictability of this policy response to industrialization has been studied and measured by economists. One 1986 study of protection offered to farm sectors across the industrial world, by economists Masayoshi Honma and Yujiro Hayami, found that 60 to 70 percent of all variations in the protection level given to farmers could be explained solely through reference to the comparative advantage lost by the agricultural sector relative to the industrial sector.

Do farmers in rich countries need subsidies to survive?

When farm subsidies were initiated in the United States in 1933, most farmers were relatively poor, with average income less than half that of non-farmers. At this point, in the depths of the Great Depression, subsidies to farmers had some economic and social justification. The justification began to diminish, however, when millions of poor farmers left the land during and after World War II, taking higher paying jobs in urban industry. The result was a consolidation of farms into much larger and more productive units, with most no longer needing subsidies to prosper. Thanks to farm consolidations, the greatest share of all food production in America today comes from very large commercial farmers who enjoy average incomes that would be significantly higher than the non-farm average even without subsidies. Their average net worth is higher still, because of the valuable land, buildings, and machinery they own. As of 2007, according to USDA surveys, more than half of all farm production in the United States came from very large family farms with annual product sales greater than $500,000, an average household income of $268,000, and an average net worth of $2.5 million. Despite the large scale of commercial farm operations in the United States, family ownership remains the norm; only 18 percent of farm production in the United States comes from farms that are not family owned.

Large commercial farmers do not need subsidies to remain prosperous, yet they continue to get the largest share of the subsidies. Most farm subsidies remain linked to current or past production volume, so the biggest farms get the biggest subsidies. In the United States in 2007, the very large farms that generated 53 percent of production were only 5 percent of all farms, but they received 45 percent of all agricultural subsidies. In Europe, the wealthiest 20 percent of farmers typically receive over 80 percent of the subsidies.

Efforts to improve the targeting of subsidy payments are routinely blocked by lobbyists representing commercial farmers. In 2008 President George W. Bush proposed to Congress that the law should be changed to prevent the delivery of some subsidy payments to farmers who earned more than $200,000, but the Senate voted that the cap should instead be set at $750,000, and the House of Representatives said there should be no cap at all.

Why are farm subsidies hard to cut?

Non-farmers outnumber farmers by at least 20 to 1 in most rich countries, yet they seldom mount effective campaigns to cut farm subsidies. In part this is because city people respect the heritage of farming and want to help those working on the land, and also because few have any idea how poorly targeted the subsidies are. In addition, smaller numbers of farmers find it easier to organize for political action than very large numbers of consumers and taxpayers, according to the "logic of collective action" originally spelled out by economist Mancur Olson. Very large groups (like food consumers) find it hard to organize because non-participation is harder to notice and police. For the same reason, some smaller commodity groups (e.g., sugar farmers) do better at getting subsidies than larger commodity groups, such as wheat or soybean farmers.

Also, as the total number of farmers continues to shrink with industrial development, the average benefit *per farmer* can continue going up without generating higher budget costs overall. Moreover, if the budget cost of farm support does increase in a wealthy country, it may not be noticed alongside the rising costs of much larger budget items, such as health care costs or defense spending. Finally, when farm supports make food more expensive in rich countries, consumers will tend not to notice because food spending will still be falling relative to income. The average share of personal income spent on food in the United States has fallen from 41 percent a century ago to just 10 percent today. This drop would have been even greater without farm income support programs, but this is something consumers do not know, or at least it is something they do not notice.

Despite these powerful political forces that tend to keep subsidies in place, once the farming share of the national workforce shrinks to a small enough size (below about 5 percent), the level of support given to farmers will usually reach a peak and begin to decline. At this point, the number of farmers will become too small, and their prosperity too conspicuous, to sustain a continued growth in support. This is now happening in both Europe and the United States. Between 2000 and 2011, the annual amount of income transferred to farmers through government programs in Europe declined by 21 percent, and in the United States by 40 percent. This decline also reflected an emergence of higher commodity prices, since farm subsidy programs that are linked to crop prices will automatically shrink when commodity prices rise, as they did particularly after 2007.

What is the "farm bill" and what is the "farm lobby"?

The legislative package that renews America's farm subsidy entitlement system roughly every five years is known as the "farm bill," and the organized groups that promote the subsidies in this bill are known as the "farm lobby." Passage of the farm bill is a process controlled almost entirely by Congress. President George W. Bush tried to veto the 2008 farm bill because it carried a five-year budget cost of $286 billion that he considered wasteful, but Congress easily overrode his veto, by margins of 316–108 votes in the House and 82–13 votes in the Senate.

The secret to every farm bill's success in Congress is the lead role played by the Agricultural Committees of the House and the Senate, where members from farm states enjoy a dominant presence and are rewarded for their efforts with generous campaign contributions from organizations representing the farmers who get the subsidies. The Agriculture Committees draft the legislation that later goes to the floor for a final vote, and in the drafting process they take care to satisfy the minimum needs of both Republican and Democratic members, ensuring bipartisan support within the committee. The farm bill enacted in 2002 actually passed the House Agriculture Committee without a single dissenting vote. The drafters also give generous treatment both to Northern crops (such as wheat and corn) and Southern crops (such as cotton and rice), and they take care to include generous funding for domestic food and nutrition programs (like the "Food Stamp" program, now called SNAP) to lock in support from urban district members. Then they add some measures to please environmentalists, such as a "Conservation Reserve" program that pays farmers to leave their land (temporarily) idle. The final package becomes impossible to stop; it is what students of legislative politics call a "committee-based logroll."

Once the farm bill leaves the committees and reaches the floor, classic vote trading will then push it toward successful enactment: farm state members implicitly or explicitly promise that they will vote for future measures of interest to non-farm members. For urban and suburban members, a single "aye" vote on the farm bill once every five years pays off when their own pet projects later come up for a vote.

This farm subsidy renewal process is supported by a formidable nexus of institutions often referred to as an "iron triangle." At the congressional corner of the triangle are the House and Senate Agriculture Committees, populated and chaired by strong farm subsidy advocates. At the Executive Branch corner is the United States Department of Agriculture (USDA), which administers the subsidy programs and values them to protect the department from diminished relevance in a post-agricultural age. At the third corner are the private farm lobby organizations. The best-known of these are two "general" farm organizations, the American Farm Bureau Federation (commonly known as the Farm Bureau), which represents the interests of large commercial farmers, mostly Republicans, and the National Farmers Union, which represents the interests of smaller farmers, mostly Democrats. When it comes to shaping the details of the farm bill, however, the most influential private lobby organizations are those representing individual commodity producer groups, such as the National Corn Growers Association, the U.S. Wheat Associates, the National Cotton Council of America, or the National Milk Producers Federation. These organizations contribute to the reelection campaigns of their favorite Agriculture Committee members, then send their skilled and always affable operatives to work the committee rooms and halls of Congress during the legislative drafting process.

The continuing clout of the farm lobby was clearly visible in the outcome of the 2008 farm bill debate, which took place at a time when most of America's farmers were enjoying enormous prosperity thanks to the highest market prices for farm commodities seen in more than three decades. Net farm income in 2008 reached $89 billion, 40 percent above the average of the previous ten years. Yet the farm lobby asserted that American agriculture was facing "emergencies" of various kinds and needed a new "safety net" for protection. The 2008 bill thus included added spending for research on organic agriculture and specialty crops, new conservation measures, block grants to promote horticultural products, and a new Average Crop Revenue Election (ACRE) program.

This routine renewal of farm subsidies proved more difficult in 2012, when the Republican leadership of the House of Representatives prevented legislation from coming to a floor vote. This happened partly out of embarrassment that the agriculture committee had proposed only a 3.5 percent spending cut in the middle of an extreme budget crisis. Direct payments to farmers would have been ended under the draft legislation, and the SNAP (food stamp) program would be cut slightly, but much of the money saved would go into more generous subsidies for crop insurance, a newly popular measure with farmers following the 2012 drought. In the end, voting for a new farm bill was postponed until some time in 2013, as part of a larger congressional deal over the so-called 'fiscal cliff.' This meant that in the short term existing subsidies would be extended with no cuts at all. In 2011 and 2012, farm income levels in the United States were the highest and second highest on record and would have been so even without subsidies—yet the subsidies were not taken away.

Is the use of corn for ethanol a subsidy to farmers?

Agricultural crops such as sugar or corn can be fermented to produce ethyl alcohol (ethanol), which is then blended with gasoline for use as an automobile fuel. Beginning in 1978,

Congress began promoting the use of corn for fuel by providing tax credits to those that blended ethanol with gasoline, and by setting in place tariffs to block the import of cheaper sugar-based ethanol from Brazil and the Caribbean. The promotion of corn-based ethanol was then ramped up under the Energy Independence and Security Act of 2007, when Congress added a quantitative mandate that ethanol use from products like corn should total at least 15 billion gallons by 2015. The ostensible purpose of this new Renewable Fuel Standard (RFS) was to reduce America's dependence on imported oil for reasons of national security, but there were also clear financial benefits to the ethanol industry and corn growers, both of which were strong advocates for these measures.

The new government mandate helped to trigger a dramatic expansion of the ethanol industry in the United States, accompanied by an increasing diversion of corn into fuel production. Between 1983 and 2010, ethanol production jumped from 2.8 billion gallons to 13 billion gallons, and by 2012, the percentage of America's corn harvest processed in ethanol distilleries had reached an astonishing 40 percent (however, about one-third of what is processed returns to the agricultural market as high protein feed for animals). Some of this diversion of agricultural crops to fuel use would have taken place even without government subsidies and mandates, given the higher market price for petroleum after 2005. When petroleum prices are high and corn prices are low, market forces alone will divert more corn into use as a feedstock for fuel. The subsidies and mandates undeniably accelerated the growth of a corn-based ethanol industry in the United States, but if the price of oil goes high enough, the ethanol industry will expand even without government props.

What is the value of promoting corn-based ethanol in the United States?

Corn-based ethanol can sometimes makes commercial sense, but on energy security and environmental grounds it makes very little sense. In the search for national energy independence, ethanol from corn can never offer more than a small gain. According to one 2007 study in the journal *Regulation*, even if 100 percent of United States corn production were processed for ethanol, the total share of national gasoline consumption displaced would be just 3.5 percent.

The environmental consequences of switching from fossil fuels to corn-based ethanol are also unappealing, in part because fossil fuels must be burned while planting, harvesting, and processing the corn, as well as to manufacture the required fertilizers. Growing more corn for use as fuel also has adverse land-use implications. A 2008 study by Joe Fargioine in the journal *Science* concluded that when worldwide land-use changes are taken into account, the greenhouse gas emissions from first producing and then burning corn-based ethanol are greater than those from producing and burning gasoline. It makes greater environmental sense, and also greater commercial sense, to burn ethanol that has been produced from sugar rather than corn, yet policy in the United States promotes ethanol from corn, because corn is what American farms produce.

Nonetheless, the politics of ethanol changed in the United States in 2011, in part because the $6 billion annual budget cost of the blending tax credit had become harder for Congress to justify in the face of Tea Party criticism of deficit spending, and also in part because with the mandate in place—and with continued high petroleum prices—the tax credit was no longer necessary to preserve the industry. In addition, shale gas production was reducing America's need for energy imports, so the national security argument was less urgent. As a consequence, Congress allowed both the tax credit to blenders and the tariff on imported ethanol to expire in 2011.

The RFS mandates remained in place, but then in the summer of 2012, a severe drought hit the corn-growing regions of the United States, pushing corn prices up to more than 8 dollars a bushel, which damaged livestock producers who purchase corn for feed. By August 2012, more than 150 members of Congress were supporting a request to the Environmental Protection Agency (EPA) to waive the RFS mandate for ethanol production. The EPA decided to keep the mandate in place, since for the moment blenders could meet the requirement by using credits saved up from having exceeded mandate levels in previous years.

The story became more complicated in 2013, when a federal appeals court threw out the part of the RFS that had mandated blenders to use woody crops and wastes as advanced "second generation" feedstocks, a decision that increased the attraction of using imported sugar-based ethanol from Brazil to meet the advanced feedstock requirements, not an outcome the original authors of the mandate would have desired.

How do farm subsidies shape international agricultural trade?

The farm subsidies of rich countries have long distorted both production and trade. They cause too much food to be produced in regions not well suited to farming, such as alpine countries in Europe, or desert lands in the American Southwest, or the municipal suburbs of Japan, and too little in the developing countries of the tropics where agricultural potential is often far greater. Farm subsidies in the United States, Europe, and Japan also tend to take market shares away from other rich countries with more advantaged farming assets, such as Australia or New Zealand. Sugar markets are one example. Because of the guarantees of high sugar prices still being provided through import restrictions in both Europe and the United States, too much of the world's sugar production comes from the growing of sugar beets inside these two markets rather than from sugarcane in the Caribbean, Brazil, or tropical Africa. D. Gale Johnson, a respected agricultural economist, once calculated that because of protectionist farm subsidy policies at least 40 percent of the world's sugar crop was being grown in the wrong place.

When international prices are trending downward, as they were prior to 2005, these distortions impose measurable hardships on farmers in the developing world. In 2002, the Brazilian government raised a formal complaint against American cotton subsidies, showing that without those subsidies production in the United States would have been 29 percent lower, cotton exports from the United States would have been 41 percent lower, and international cotton prices for Brazilian producers would have been 13 percent higher. This would have brought benefits not only to Brazil but also to small cotton farmers in West Africa, many of whom live on less than $1 a day. According to calculations commissioned by Oxfam America, if United States cotton programs had been eliminated in 2005, and if the international price of cotton had consequently increased by 6–14 percent, eight very poor countries in West Africa would have been able to earn an additional $191 million each year in foreign exchange from their cotton exports, and household income in these countries would have increased by 2.3 to 5.7 percent.

Has the WTO been able to discipline farm subsidies?

One purpose of the World Trade Organization (WTO) has been to reduce trade distortions caused by subsidies, yet successive rounds of multilateral trade negotiations in the WTO (and within its predecessor organization, the General Agreement on Tariffs and Trade, or GATT) have made only modest progress in achieving this goal. Agricultural tariffs around the world still average 62 percent, compared to just 4 percent for manufactured goods. Agricultural tariffs in the United States average 12 percent, in the EU 30 percent, and in Japan 50 percent. In many developing countries, tariffs are even higher. In India, for example, the average bound tariff on agricultural goods is 114 percent.

Barriers to international agricultural trade are difficult to bring down in rich countries because without those barriers domestic farm support policies would be far more expensive for governments to operate. In Europe and Japan, it is politically easy to transfer income to farmers through trade restrictions at the border because these do not cost anything in budget terms (they may actually earn tariff revenue for the government) and they push costs onto foreign producers (who complain, but cannot vote). In poor countries, meanwhile, barriers to agricultural trade are hard to bring down because they frequently reflect a political desire for "self-sufficiency" in staple food supplies. Even when their own people are not well fed, and even when prices on the world market may be lower than the domestic price, governments in many developing countries have traditionally preferred not to import staple foods.

Within the WTO, a distinction has emerged between subsidies to farmers that distort production (and hence trade) versus those that do not. The most recent WTO strategy has been for governments to negotiate limits on trade-distorting subsidies only, while providing unlimited cash subsidies to farmers so long as those payments are "decoupled" from any incentive to produce more. Payments that supposedly do not incentivize new production are placed in a "Green Box," while policies that clearly distort production are placed either in a "Red Box" (they are banned) or in an "Amber Box" (where they are allowed, but only up to a certain dollar value). Following this approach in the Uruguay Round of WTO negotiations that ended in 1993, the United States and Europe were able to agree to reduce their Amber Box supports by 20 percent from a 1986 baseline. Following this agreement, both the United States and the EU voluntarily decoupled larger portions of their farm subsidy budgets, so they could be moved into the Green Box and increased without WTO restriction.

Even with this Green Box loophole in place (plus a second, more dubious loophole known as the Blue Box), it proved impossible after 2001 to reach a follow-up agricultural agreement in the next round of WTO negotiations. This Doha Round was suspended without a result in the summer of 2008. It should have been much easier by 2008 to reach an international agreement to lower trade-distorting farm subsidies, since much higher international food prices were then making the subsidies less essential as a tool for supporting domestic farm income. In the Doha negotiations the U.S. Trade Representative offered to accept a much lower cap on U.S. Amber Box subsidies, just $14.5 billion. This did not alarm farmers because due to high prices actual trade distorting subsidies had fallen to a level well below that figure. The talks nonetheless collapsed without a result when some developing countries—including both China and India—said no. They had concluded that the new access they might gain to agricultural markets in the United States and the European Union would not be enough to justify the new concessions they were being asked to make in opening their own domestic markets for both agricultural and manufacturing goods. Agreements in the World Trade Organization must be reached on a "consensus" basis, making them more difficult to reach as the number of major economic powers has increased. The emergence of Brazil, India, and China as stronger economic powers in recent years has made the task of reaching a multilateral consensus on agriculture in the WTO far more daunting.

Do trade agreements like NAFTA hurt farmers in countries like Mexico?

When global negotiations in the WTO stall, the United States often attempts to open markets abroad through regional or bilateral trade agreements. In his 2013 State of the Union address, President Obama even signaled a desire to negotiate a Transatlantic Free-Trade Agreement (TAFTA), parallel to a possible Trans-Pacific Partnership (TPP) free trade agreement. Securing European Union (EU) or Japanese support for this approach might require a "carve out" provision for agriculture to limit or perhaps even exclude reductions in farm subsidies.

One regional free trade agreement that did not carve out agriculture was the North American Free Trade Agreement (NAFTA), completed in 1993. This agreement triggered a significant phase-out of agricultural import barriers between the United States and Mexico. For this reason NAFTA was strongly opposed by anti-globalization advocacy groups who argue that the agreement hurt poor corn farmers in Mexico by exposing them to a flood of cheap imports of corn from subsidized growers in the United States. This is offered as one reason so many Mexican farmers have left the land and moved into urban slums.

Reviewing actual experience since 1993, Mexico did import much more corn from the United States after NAFTA, but this was mostly yellow corn for animal feed to support expanding hog and poultry production, not the white corn for tortillas grown by poor farmers in Mexico. Corn production inside Mexico itself actually continued to increase, despite higher imports, in part because commercial corn growers in Mexico were also getting subsidies (37 percent of the income of Mexican corn growers came from government supports in 2002, compared to 26 percent in the United States). A review of academic studies done by the World Bank in 2004 concluded that the decline of Mexican white corn prices was actually a long-term trend that preceded NAFTA. This study found that the U.S.-Mexico producer price differential for maize did not change significantly after NAFTA came into effect in 1994.

Lowering import restrictions for basic food staples can nonetheless be a risky policy for some developing countries. Haiti was self-sufficient in rice in the 1970s and 1980s, but in the 1990s it reduced its import tariffs from 50 percent to just 3 percent, allowing less expensive rice from the United States to flood in. Eventually, Haiti was importing 80 percent of its rice and, partly because of lower prices, domestic production was stagnant. Then came the international price spike of 2008, which brought a tripling of the import price, followed by riots in the streets of Port-au-Prince. In 2010, former U.S. president

Bill Clinton, who was from the rice-growing state of Arkansas, apologized for having supported a set of subsidy and trade policies that helped big farmers in the United States while undercutting small rice producers in Haiti, calling this a "devil's bargain."

9

FARMING, THE ENVIRONMENT, CLIMATE CHANGE, AND WATER

Does agriculture always damage the environment?

From the perspective of deep ecology, all forms of agriculture damage the natural environment. When our early ancestors went from hunting and gathering to planting crops and grazing animals, they cut forests and redirected waterways. Wild plants and animals were domesticated, then progressively modified through selective breeding. If protecting nature is the central goal, these actions must be considered damage. Using a more utilitarian and socially centered perspective, however, changes to nature caused by farming would be viewed as damage only if they brought long-term costs to human society that exceed the short-term food production gain. Even if we use this more forgiving definition, many kinds of farming today do damage the environment.

It is useful to classify the environmental damage done by farming according to where it takes place: on the farm versus off the farm. Farmers themselves will suffer most from damage on the farm, while it is mostly non-farmers who suffer if the damage is off the farm and downstream. In an important way, politics sets the balance between these two kinds of damage. Farmers in poor countries lack political power, so they will often find themselves trapped into using practices that damage their own farm resource base, and hence their own livelihood. Farmers in rich countries have considerable organized political power, so they will find it easier both to protect their own resource base and to get away with actions that pollute air and water downstream from farms, to the disadvantage of non-farmers.

In the poorest developing countries, most of the environmental damage done by agriculture takes place on the farm itself. Prime examples include the exhaustion of soil nutrients due to shortened fallow times, waterlogging of soils due to mismanaged irrigation, or the "desertification" of rangeland caused by excessive animal grazing. By harming the agricultural resource base itself, this sort of damage lowers productivity and helps keep farmers poor. Research presented at an Africa Fertilizer Summit in 2006 revealed that the shortening of fallow times in Africa was removing nitrogen from the soil at an average annual rate of 22–26 kilograms per hectare, far too much to be offset by current rates of fertilizer application, which average only 9 kilograms per hectare. The result of this "soil mining" was a deficit in soil nutrients that causes annual crop losses estimated at between $1 billion and $3 billion. Nor is this the end of the problem. As cultivated soils become exhausted, farmers will extend cropping onto new lands, cutting more trees and destroying more wildlife habitat. According to the World Resources Institute, land clearing for the expansion of unsustainable low-yield farming has caused roughly 70 percent of all deforestation in Africa.

In wealthy industrial societies, by contrast, environmental damage from farming usually results from too much input use rather than too little, and those who suffer most are usually not farmers. For example, excessive nitrogen fertilizer use leads to nitrate runoff and eutrophication of streams and ponds. In Europe, excess nitrates in water are a downstream health hazard ("blue baby syndrome"). In the United States, excessive nitrogen fertilizer use on farms in the Mississippi River watershed contributes to an environmental calamity both within that watershed and also in the Gulf of Mexico, where a 6,000-square-mile "dead zone" is no longer able to support aquatic life. In the Florida Everglades, nitrogen and phosphorous runoff from sugarcane production has produced cattail growth so thick as to replace the native sawgrass, ruining the habitat of wading birds like storks, and then sucking oxygen from the water when the cattails die and decompose, which kills the fish.

Exploitation of river water for crop irrigation can harm migratory fish species, such as salmon, which are unable to move upstream through the narrow passages and turbines of dams. Concentrated animal feeding operations (CAFOs), designed to cut livestock industry costs by fattening thousands of animals for slaughter all within one crowded facility, often pollute both the air and water with toxic effluents, creating health risks for non-farming human populations living nearby. The poultry industry in just a single county in Delaware produces 200 million birds a year, and mishandled chicken waste has been a major source of eutrophication in the Chesapeake Bay.

What kind of farming is environmentally sustainable?

Environmental activists and agricultural scientists answer this question in dramatically different ways. Environmentalists usually prefer small-scale diversified farming systems that rely on fewer inputs purchased off the farm, and on systems that imitate nature rather than trying to engineer or dominate nature. Agricultural scientists tend to assume that there will be less harm done to nature overall by moving toward specialized high-yield farming systems employing the latest technology, because increasing crop yields on lands already farmed will allow more of the remaining land to be saved for nature. While environmentalists invoke the damage done by modern farming, agricultural scientists invoke the greater damage that would be done if the same volume of production had to come from low-yield farming systems.

The environmentalist side of this argument was most eloquently presented in 1962 in Rachel Carson's landmark book, *Silent Spring*, which exposed the damage done by chemical pesticides both to human health and to wild animal species (including songbirds, hence the title). Carson's book led to a legal ban on the agricultural use of DDT in the United States and also to the formation of a broad and powerful environmental movement, which in 1970 secured passage of the National Environmental Protection Act, creating America's Environmental Protection Agency (EPA). Carson's thinking also reinforced a continuing quest among environmentalists for an alternative to high-input, high-yield farming.

One early pioneer in this search for "alternative" models of farming was Wes Jackson, who founded a Land Institute in Kansas in 1976, to promote farming based on polycultures of perennial crops rather than monocultures of annual crops. This approach did not prove to be a commercial success, but it was Jackson, in 1980, who began employing the term "sustainable agriculture" to describe his objectives. Responding to political interest in alternative farming systems, the Department of Agriculture in 1985 finally initiated a program to promote what it called low-impact sustainable agriculture, or LISA. Conventional commercial farmers panned it as "low income sustainable agriculture," but the idea gained traction with non-farming urban populations and with a younger cohort of countercultural farmers who had links to a back-to-the-land movement from the 1960s.

High-input farming did cause environmental damage in America during the second half of the twentieth century, but the earlier style of low-input farming had also been damaging. It was an extension of low-yield wheat farming into the southern plains of Kansas, Oklahoma, and the Texas panhandle in the 1920s, before synthetic chemical fertilizers or pesticides were in wide use, that produced America's single greatest environmental disaster until that time, a drought-induced loss of topsoil that ruined farmlands across an area as big as the state of Pennsylvania, turning it into a "dust bowl." Roughly 400,000 farmers fled the dust bowl, many of them moving to California to work as migrants picking tomatoes and peas, a flow of environmental refugees unmatched in scale until Hurricane Katrina subsequently flooded out the population of New Orleans in 2005.

Following Carson's book, while environmentalists were concluding that chemical use to increase crop yields was inherently dangerous, commercial farmers and agricultural scientists sought instead to develop new chemicals that were less harmful and ways to apply them with greater precision to reduce runoff. Environmental advocates were not impressed with this "technical fix" approach; they wanted a more complete move away from highly specialized, highly capitalized "industrial" farming. Their views were later supported by a 2008 International Assessment of Agricultural Science and Technology for Development (IAASTD), which warned that using still more modern science to "increase yields and productivity" might do even more environmental damage.

Growing numbers of popular writers have embraced this view. In an apocalyptic 2008 book titled *The End of Food*, journalist Paul Roberts argued that the world's large-scale, hyper-efficient industrialized food production systems were heading toward an inevitable collapse because of the damage they had been doing to soils, water systems, and other "natural infrastructure." Alternative food advocate Michael Pollan wrote in 2008 that "the era of cheap and abundant food appears to be drawing to a close." In 2013, *New York Times* food columnist Mark Bittman described America's "hyper-industrial" agricultural system as having poisoned land and water, wasted energy, and made a major contribution to climate change. "We must figure out a way to un-invent this food system," said Bittman. Despite such popular sentiments, a preponderance of agricultural scientists and economists do not reject today's large-scale, specialized, and highly capitalized farming systems as unsustainable. In fact, they view these systems as the best means available to contain environmental damage from farming.

What is low-impact or "precision" farming?

Commercial farming today has moved well beyond the indiscriminate chemical use practices that Rachel Carson properly criticized in 1962. Many of the early insecticides then in use have now been banned and replaced by chemicals that are less persistent in the environment and effective when applied in lower volume. Commercial farmers are always looking for ways to cut back on unnecessary chemical and fuel use so as to reduce costs, and by the end of the twentieth century they had found a number of technical means to do so. These new methods came to be labeled "precision" farming.

Beginning in the 1970s and 1980s, during an interlude of extremely high energy prices, farmers in the United States first learned to save diesel fuel by planting seeds in unplowed fields—a "no-till" approach to farming that also reduced erosion, conserved soil moisture, and sequestered carbon. They also switched from flood irrigation to less wasteful center-pivot sprays, or to laser-leveled fields with zero runoff, and to even more precise drip irrigation systems. Then, in the 1990s, they began using Global Positioning Systems (GPS) to auto-steer tractors in perfectly straight lines with zero overlap (saving more diesel fuel), plus soil-mapping and onboard computer systems to match chemical applications of fertilizer or lime more precisely to location-specific needs. The GPS told them exactly where they were in a field to within one square meter, and with variable rate application machinery they could deliver precisely the amount of water or fertilizer required in that part of the field. Infrared sensors can be used to detect the greenness of a crop, telling a farmer exactly how much more (or less) fertilizer might be needed. To minimize nitrogen runoff, fertilizer can also be inserted into the soil in much smaller total quantities at exactly the depth of the plant roots, and in perfect rows exactly where the seeds will be planted. Also in the 1990s, farmers in the United States began planting genetically engineered soybean, corn, and cotton seeds that made it possible to control weeds without mechanical tillage and to control insects without as many chemical sprays.

Farmers took up these more precise methods to save money on chemicals, water, and diesel fuel, but the side result was a clear benefit to the environment. American agricultural output has increased by 40 percent since the early 1980s, but chemical fertilizer use, insecticide use, and herbicide use have all declined in absolute terms. Energy use, land use, and water use have declined most conspicuously on a per bushel of production basis. Department of Agriculture surveys reveal that between 1980 and 2011, energy use per bushel of corn production fell 43 percent. Land use per bushel fell 30 percent. Soil erosion per bushel fell 67 percent. Irrigation water use per bushel fell 53 percent. And greenhouse gas emissions per bushel fell 36 percent.

The United States has not been alone in making this technical move in commercial farming toward reduced input use per bushel of production. In 2008 the Organisation for Economic Co-operation and Development (OECD) in Paris published an important review of the "environmental performance of agriculture" in the 30 most advanced industrial countries of the world (those with the most highly capitalized farming systems). The new data showed that between 1990 and 2004, total food production in these countries increased in volume by 5 percent from an already high level, yet adverse environmental impacts had diminished in nearly every category. The area of land taken up by agriculture declined 4 percent. Soil erosion from both wind and water was reduced. Water use on irrigated lands declined by 9 percent. Energy use on the farm increased at only one-sixth the rate of energy use in the rest of the economy. Gross greenhouse gas emissions from farming fell by 3 percent. Herbicide and insecticide spraying declined by 5 percent. Excessive nitrogen fertilizer use declined by 17 percent. Biodiversity also improved, as increased numbers of crop varieties and livestock breeds came into use.

True believers in the promise of precision farming expect there will be no end to the impact-reducing gains that can be achieved. Their long-term vision includes small solar-powered robots working farm fields in groups, hoeing weeds and picking off bugs 24 hours a day without any polluting chemicals or fossil fuels at all, then harvesting the crop with almost no human supervision required. Even if this fantasy became possible, most environmental advocates would refuse to see it as progress. They generally do not endorse modern precision farming because it favors highly capitalized industrial-scale operations, something they reject on principle. The small, diversified farms they favor cannot make use of the costly and specialized machinery that is a key component to most modern precision farming. In addition, environmental advocates instinctively reject the notion that a biological system such as a farm can be sustainably and safely precision-engineered through science. They believe, with Rachel Carson, that nature will always find a way to strike back against human arrogance of this kind.

Do fragile lands, population growth, and poverty make farming unsustainable?

These are popular explanations for environmental damage from farming, but institutional arrangements are usually more important.

The concept of "fragile" land can be misleading. It is true that many poor countries farm on sloping lands or irregular lands with thin and badly weathered soils, all subject to the damaging extremes of heat, flood, and drought. In many tropical countries, soil nutrients leach away immediately when trees are cut, leaving a baked and barren landscape on which only weeds will grow. Under proper management, however, these less productive tropical lands can be improved dramatically and farmed sustainably. When farmed with adequate fallow time, or limed to the correct acidity, or terraced and mulched to capture and keep more moisture on leveled soil, or planted to several different crops at the same time (intercropped) to reduce vulnerability to pests, the productive potential of such less-favored lands can be sustainably increased.

Some argue that poverty itself is a cause of environmental damage in farming, because poor farmers who live from hand to mouth cannot afford to wait for resource-protecting investments to pay off. Yet many poor farming communities do invest to protect their resources, if the political and institutional circumstances are right. They are more than willing to build and maintain terraces, plant trees, and protect rangelands from overgrazing when effective "common property resource" (CPR) systems are allowed to operate at the local or village level. These informal systems protect local forests, streams, ponds, and grazing lands by allocating equitable use to insiders while denying access to outsiders. Such systems are good at blocking the "tragedy of the commons," a pattern of environmental destruction that arises in systems of open access (Garrett Hardin, the influential ecologist who named this danger in 1968, should have called it the "tragedy of open access"). Within a well-managed commons systems, even poor communities can avoid environmental tragedies.

Commons systems are vulnerable to breakdown, however, if powerful outside institutions, such as colonial administrators, international companies, forestry department bureaucrats, megaproject engineers, government land-titling agencies, or centralized irrigation authorities, move in to take control away from local community leaders. Local farmers who sense that they are about to lose control of their resource base will at that point stop making investments in resource protection. They will begin using up the resource base as fast as they can—cutting the trees, plowing up terraces, over-grazing the range, over-fishing the ponds—before the outsiders take it away. I farmers who have control as well as access can be conserving farmers; if control is taken away, they will use their access to exploit rather than conserve.

Well-functioning common property systems in poor countries can also break down if local leaders become corrupt, or due to excess population growth. If population density increases beyond a certain point, the value per person of protecting the resource will decline so much for insiders as to demotivate efforts at protection, just when more outsiders will be attempting to gain access. At this point, effective resource protection can require switching to an individual private property system, one that restores individual payoffs for resource-protecting actions while handing the problem of excluding outsiders over to the police. If this transition to individual land ownership is made successfully, a further increase in population density need not threaten the resource base at all. In fact, greater population density makes affordable greater labor investment in protecting the land (mulching, terracing, etc.) and increases the affordability of productivity-enhancing investments in rural roads, power, and irrigation. One example from Africa is the experience of Machakos District in Kenya, where farmers in this densely settled semi-arid area avoided serious damage to their marginal soil endowments even as population increased. This occurred thanks to clearly titled land ownership that motivated heavier labor investments in terracing systems, use of more fertilizer, and a shift to higher-value crops for sale in nearby urban markets.

Do cash crops and export crops cause environmental harm?

Shifting from food crop production to a more specialized cash crop production for export is frequently cited as a cause of both economic dependency and environmental harm. There are some cases that support this generalization, for example in Central America in the 1960s and 1970s, when landlords introduced chemical-intensive cotton production and evicted traditional peasants growing maize and beans. Yet the cash crop versus food crop dichotomy is usually misleading, because a number of food crops in the developing world are at the same time cash crops (for example, rice in Asia), and many cash export crops (such as cocoa in West Africa) are grown by small farmers in the same fields with food crops, in an environmentally friendly intercropping system.

Cash crops for export are not inherently less rewarding for small farmers to grow, or more damaging to the environment. Exported cash crops are often tree crops or perennials that provide better land cover and more stable root structures than annual food crops. In Africa, some kinds of perennial export crops—such as tea or coffee, planted along the contour of sloping lands, or oil palm planted in low-lying areas—can protect the soil much better than food crops requiring annual tillage, such as maize. At least a partial switch to higher-value cash crops helps farm families with limited land and labor earn the income they need to pay for their children's school expenses. Farmers will typically switch part of their land to cash crop production, then use some of the income to purchase improved seeds and fertilizer, allowing a simultaneous boost in food crop production on the rest of their land.

Do farm subsidies promote environmental damage in agriculture?

Yes. Most subsidy policies work by giving farmers artificially high prices for their products, which induces them to use excessive fertilizers, pesticides, and irrigation water in an effort to boost crop yields as high as possible. In Korea, where rice farmers are heavily protected (with a guaranteed price roughly five times the world market price) pesticide use is extremely high, at 12.8 kilograms per hectare. In France, where farmers have less price protection, pesticide use is less than half as high, at 4.5 kilograms per hectare. In the United States, where there is even less protection, pesticide use is only 2.3 kilograms per hectare. And in Senegal, where farmers get almost no protection at all, pesticide use averages only 0.1 kilograms per hectare. In most of Africa, farmers are often taxed rather than subsidized (a symptom of their political weakness), which frequently results in too little chemical use rather than too much. Fertilizer use in most of Africa is insufficient for replacing the soil nutrients taken up by crops.

When subsidies to farmers go up, input use often goes up in lock-step. Between 1970 and 1990 in Thailand, as income protections for farmers increased, fertilizer use per hectare increased nearly sevenfold. In Indonesia in the 1980s, where the government subsidized fertilizer purchases directly by as much as 68 percent, chemical use increased 77 percent over one five-year period. In India, when the government began to subsidize 86 percent of the electric bill for pumping irrigation water in the Punjab, groundwater tables began dropping at an unsustainable rate of about 0.8 meters a year.

In rich countries, farmers are not only powerful enough politically to demand the subsidies that encourage excessive input use, they are also powerful enough to avoid being held accountable for the resulting downstream environmental damage. Because of farm lobby strength, the air and water pollution that emanates from farms in rich countries is regulated far less than pollution from other industries. In the United States, the agricultural sector is significantly exempt from the regulatory structures of both the original Clean Air Act and Clean Water Act, because pollution from farms does not come from a "point source."

Despite the dead zone in the Gulf of Mexico, Congress does not regulate excess nitrogen runoff from farms and does not tax farm fertilizer use. Instead, it has created voluntary programs that pay farmers to take land (temporarily) out of production, or to cultivate their land in ways that reduce runoff. In 2010, these incentive-based, voluntary conservation programs operated by the U.S. Department of Agriculture (USDA) cost taxpayers $5.5 billion. Instead of using a "polluter pays" principle, the government actually pays the polluter. Even in extreme cases such as chemical pollution in the Florida Everglades from heavily subsidized sugar farming, strong regulations are routinely blocked by industry. In 1996, when Vice President Al Gore proposed taxing sugar growers to finance an Everglades clean-up project, a direct phone call from a Florida sugar baron to President Bill Clinton resulted in the tax proposal being set aside.

A more recent example of the power of U.S. agriculture to resist environmental regulation can be seen in the case of climate change policy. In 2009, when the House of Representatives passed the Waxman-Markey bill to create a cap-and-trade system to limit greenhouse gas emissions, the entire agricultural sector was left "uncapped." Instead of being subject to caps under this bill, farmers would have been entitled to profit by selling "offsets" to industries in sectors that were capped. The offset would be based on a voluntary reduction in emissions, or an increased sequestering of carbon—things a farmer might be doing anyway.

One of the few environmental policy instruments strong enough to resist the farm lobby in the United States has been the 1973 Endangered Species Act. For example, in 2008, a lawsuit filed under that act by the Natural Resources Defense Council forced the Bush administration's Fish and Wildlife Service to divert more than 150 billion gallons of water away from irrigated farming in the San Joaquin Valley, in California, so as to protect the delta smelt, an endangered 3-inch bait fish. Environmentalists know that their best chance, in a battle against farmers, is usually to move the action out of Congress and into the courts.

How will climate change affect food production?

Climate change will affect food production in complex ways, and in different ways at different latitudes. In the tropics higher temperatures will damage farming, since some crops

are already being grown near the upper range of their biological heat tolerance, but in some higher temperate zone regions
warmer weather will mean longer growing seasons, and perhaps the chance to add a second seasonal crop. Average rainfall and rainfall variability will change as well, in ways far
more difficult to predict. A warming earth will be, on average,
a wetter earth, due to accelerated ocean evaporation leading
to increased cloud formation, and this can be good for farming. Other things being equal, increased carbon dioxide (CO_2)
in the atmosphere will also help farming, since plants need to
take in CO_2. This is known as the carbon fertilization effect.
But increased atmospheric ozone, another greenhouse gas, can
slow plant growth.

In North America, longer growing seasons at upper latitudes, more rainfall overall, and greater carbon fertilization
may actually provide net benefits to farming. According to
the Intergovernmental Panel on Climate Change (IPCC), crop
yields in North America are expected to increase by 5–20 percent during the first several decades of the twenty-first century, due to climate change. At the same time, these gains will
be uneven across the region, and weather variations are likely
to be more extreme. Experts disagree on whether the 2012
summer drought in the United States was linked to long-term
climate change or to short-term factors such as a cyclical La
Niña effect.

The impacts of climate change on farming in the developing world are likely to be more damaging. One 2009 projection done by the International Food Policy Research Institute
(IFPRI) was based on a linked computer model that incorporated both a food supply-and-demand component and a
biological crop growth component, one that captured yield
changes driven by temperature changes within 281 different
spatial regions around the world. The temperature changes
expected within these spatial regions, out to the year 2050,
were calculated based on modeled scenarios generated from
the IPCC's 2007 4th Assessment Report. The results of this

exercise were alarming. Rice production in the developing world in 2050 was expected to be 14 percent lower with climate change compared to without, and wheat production in the developing world was expected to be 34 percent lower due to climate change. In South Asia, specifically, wheat production was projected to be 49 percent lower in a 2050 world with climate change, compared to a world without climate change. When IFPRI then put these projected production impacts into its economic model, it estimated the higher food prices these climate effects would generate and concluded that there would be a 23 percent increase in the numbers of malnourished children expected in 2050 in a world with climate change, compared to a world without.

Two kinds of policy response are available to this threat. One would be "prevention," in the form of a redoubled effort to slow climate change, limiting any further temperature rise to no more than 2 degrees Centigrade, by somehow keeping atmospheric concentrations of CO_2 from exceeding 450 parts per million. This, however, would require a sharp downward adjustment in current fossil fuel consumption trends for countries such as China and India, as well as the United States and Europe. Such a response is politically unlikely, because it would imply much slower economic growth, at least until the costs of wind and solar power come down. A second option, favored by IFPRI, is to recognize the high probability of future climate change and to help developing countries adapt their farming systems by making larger investments in irrigation expansion and efficiency, rural roads, and agricultural research. If an added $7 billion were properly spent every year for such purposes, the adverse impacts of climate change on food production might be offset. This is a small amount of money relative to the budgets of today's major governments (the United States spends 100 times this amount on the Defense Department every year), yet political support for spending this money in the developing world is difficult to mobilize.

Does agriculture contribute to climate change?

Agriculture globally is a major contributor to climate change. The expansion of crop farming releases CO_2 into the atmosphere when trees are cut to clear land, and also when the soil is disturbed. Heat-trapping gases are also released when fuel is burned to manufacture fertilizer, or to power farm machinery, and when rice is grown in flooded paddy fields, which give off methane gas, more than 20 times as powerful in trapping heat as CO_2. Livestock production is an even more potent source of greenhouse gas emissions, because of the clearing of lands for pasture, and also because so much crop farming today goes for animal feed purposes. Moreover, the animals themselves are a source of greenhouse gas emissions, principally in the form of methane released from the digestive processes of ruminant animals (cattle, goats, sheep) that depend on microbial fermentation of fibrous grasses and feeds, and also from animal manure, which emits gases such as methane, nitrous oxide, ammonia, and carbon dioxide. The Intergovernmental Panel on Climate Change (IPCC) reported in 2007 that the agricultural sector overall was the source of 10–12 percent of total global anthropogenic emissions of greenhouse gases. If we add emissions from fertilizer production, food transport, refrigeration, consumer practices, and waste management, somewhere between one-fifth and one-third of all greenhouse gases emitted by people come from the food and farming sector, according to a 2012 analysis from the CGIAR Research Program on Climate Change, Agriculture, and Food Security. In the United States specifically, if only on-farm emissions are considered, agriculture accounts for somewhere between 7 and 8 percent of all greenhouse gas emissions.

Calculations of this sort are contentious and sometimes flawed. For example, in 2006, the United Nations Food and Agriculture Organization (FAO) released a report titled *Livestock's Long Shadow: Environmental Issues and Options*, which estimated that livestock production worldwide was responsible all by itself for 18 percent of all human-induced greenhouse gas emissions, "a bigger share than that of transport." In generating this high percentage, the FAO followed a life cycle analysis approach that considered not just greenhouse gases from the animals themselves—including methane and nitrous oxide from the digestive systems and manure of the animals—but also emissions from a large number of associated activities such as land-use changes (converting forest to pasture), the burning of fossil fuels to produce animal feed, plus emissions from animal processing and transport. The surprising findings of the report prompted an animal welfare organization, PETA, to chide former vice president Al Gore for having failed to mention reduced meat consumption as one powerful way to prevent climate change.

It later came to light that this 2006 study was an exaggerated estimate, because it had compared a full life cycle analysis of the livestock industry to only a partial life cycle analysis of other sectors. For example, in the transport sector it counted greenhouse gas emissions from the gasoline burned by cars, but not the CO_2 emitted from factories that assembled the cars, or from the factories that manufactured the steel, glass, plastic, and rubber from which the cars were made. Authors of the FAO report conceded this flaw, but livestock industry critics continued to reference the study, and they even produced a dubious study of their own claiming that livestock were actually responsible for 51 percent of global greenhouse gas emissions.

One useful message from the original FAO study was that livestock systems based on extensive grazing are just as prone to produce greenhouse gas emissions as systems based on confined feeding. Cattle raised exclusively on grass take far longer to reach a market weight than cattle finished in a confined system, meaning more months or years of digestive methane and nitrous oxide emissions per pound of meat. As for confined systems (concentrated animal feeding operations, or CAFOs), they generate less methane and nitrous oxide per pound of meat, but usually much more CO_2, because of the diesel fuel burned in growing the feed grain.

Returning to a more traditional farm production system may seem a tempting way to reduce greenhouse gas emissions, but given today's much greater market demand for food, including animal products like meat, traditional systems would actually result in an increase in emissions. In 2010, a team of scientists at Stanford estimated that if world food consumption in 2005 had to be satisfied with the average crop yields of 1961, the total area of cropland under production worldwide would have to more than double, a damaging change in land use that would release sequestered carbon from forests and soils and increase global greenhouse gas emissions from agriculture roughly fivefold. This same study then asked how actual greenhouse gas emissions in 2005 would have changed if the world returned not only to 1961 crop yields, but also to 1961 per capita consumption levels. Moving back to a 1961 diet (one that depended far less on meat consumption) would reduce greenhouse gas emissions, but only enough to offset about half the damage done by moving back to the lower 1961 crop yields. The lesson from this study was that the worst possible situation for climate change would be a world that retains the current level of meat consumption but moves back to 1961 (pre-green revolution) crop yields.

Is the world running out of water to irrigate crops?

For farmers everywhere, water is destiny. Producing one kilogram of wheat requires the use of about 1,000 liters of water, and paddy rice requires twice this amount. The earth's freshwater supply is not diminishing overall, since it is renewed every time it rains, and about 60 percent of farm production in the developing world is still based on rainfall alone. Yet in regions where rainfall is uncertain or inadequate, irrigation techniques that bring freshwater from surface streams or from underground aquifers to the roots of crops are essential. Irrigated farming is the most reliable and often the most productive kind of farming; irrigated land makes up about one-fifth of total arable area in the developing world, yet it provides two-fifths of all crops harvested and close to three-fifths of cereal production.

Total irrigated land area has doubled over the past 50 years, and globally today about 20 percent of all cultivated land is under irrigation. Roughly 70 percent of all the water we take from aquifers, streams, and lakes now goes into agriculture. Because the most promising sites for irrigation were developed long ago, the United Nations FAO expects irrigated area to grow more slowly in the years ahead, by only 6 percent between 2009 and 2050. This may not be enough to keep pace with future production requirements.

Expanding the use of irrigation water for agriculture will be difficult for several reasons. First will be an unavoidable increase in competition for freshwater from urban users, but second will be the needless degradation of some past irrigation sites. Poor drainage of irrigated lands has left some lands waterlogged or saline. Basins of dams have silted up, reducing capacity. In many large rivers, excessive withdrawals have left as little as 5 percent of the former water volume instream, and some rivers no longer reach the sea year-round. Nearly 40 percent of irrigated area now depends primarily on groundwater, yet aquifer depletion is a growing threat because rates of pumping have proved nearly impossible to regulate. According to one 2012 estimate published in *Nature*, roughly 1.7 billion people now live in areas where groundwater resources or groundwater-dependent ecosystems are under threat.

What can be done to improve water management in farming?

The first and most important step is to reduce water waste. The technical means available include shifting from flood irrigation to more precise spray-and-drip systems, leveling fields to eliminate runoff, and lining irrigation canals to reduce seepage. The policy steps needed include ending subsidies for cheap electricity that encourage excessive pumping (in India, for example), establishing water users' associations to regulate access, and creating water markets based on tradeable water rights.

Private water markets have saved farming in some dry parts of Australia. One example is the Murray-Darling Basin, where the Australian government in the 1990s shifted from building dams and subsidizing water to a policy that separated water rights from land rights. This allowed farmers with less need for water to sell their rights to farmers who needed more. Total water availability was falling in this basin, yet the income of farmers remained high, thanks to the operation of this water market. As water availability went down, the price of water went up, which encouraged growers of thirsty low-value crops such as rice to sell some of their water rights to growers of higher-value crops such as vegetables or grapes. The system allows willing buyers and willing sellers to make deals, which in the end allocate scarce water to its highest value use. Water trading systems for farmers also operate at the state level in the western part of the United States, in Arizona, New Mexico, Colorado, and California.

While reducing water waste in currently irrigated regions, it will be equally important in the years ahead to extend irrigation coverage to regions where rainfall alone does not allow crop farmers to prosper. In Africa today, only 4 percent of cultivated land is irrigated, and 41 percent of annual farm production comes from lands that are both hot and dry. Farmers on these dry lands are pushed back into poverty every time the rains fail. The irregular topography of much of Africa, plus poor rural road and power infrastructures, have discouraged investments in irrigation. Building dams also encounters opposition from environmental groups. Because so many non-governmental organizations (NGOs) are now opposed to dams, the World Bank has virtually stopped financing such projects in the developing world. NGOs tend to favor small-scale irrigation alternatives such as rainwater harvesting, bucket irrigation, treadle and pedal pumps, and small earthen dams, yet these options are hard to scale up and they carry excessive labor costs in much of rural Africa.

Citizens in today's rich countries, who gained prosperity in part by building dams to develop 70 percent or more of their own hydroelectric potential, might wish to think twice about telling Africa—where only 3 percent of potential has so far been developed—that dams are a bad idea.

10

LIVESTOCK, MEAT, AND FISH

How are farm animals different from crops?

In some respects, they are not so different. Human beings have eaten animals—including fish—from the beginning, and we have bred domesticated animals to serve our food purposes in much the way that we have bred crops. Moreover, market forces are pushing modern livestock production systems and modern crop production systems in roughly the same direction, toward increased specialization, automation, capital investment, and much larger scale. Consumer prices for animal products have consequently fallen over the long term, once again parallel to the long-term decline in crop prices.

In at least three respects, however, farm animals are significantly different from farm crops. First, and most obviously, they require more intensive management at a much higher ethical standard, because unlike plants they move about when not confined and maintain complex social and emotional lives. Second, farm animals must themselves be given food, often in large amounts, making the food products we derive from animals more expensive. Third, farm animals produce manure, which is a valuable product for restoring soil nutrients if managed properly; if mismanaged, however, it becomes a human health hazard and a damaging source of water and air pollution.

Is meat consumption increasing, or not?

Globally, meat consumption has been increasing at a rapid rate, tripling over the past 50 years. To sustain this higher consumption, herders and livestock producers around the world are now managing more than 26 billion animals at any one time, triple the 1970 number. The earth, in other words, is now supporting four times as many agricultural animals as people.

The driving factor behind this global increase in raising animals for food has been personal income growth. As societies become more wealthy, people almost invariably use a part of the higher income to purchase more meat, milk, and eggs. In wealthy regions such as Europe and North America, average annual per capita meat consumption has reached as high as 83 kilograms, far more than in less wealthy regions such as Latin America (58 kilograms), East Asia and the Pacific (28 kilograms), or Sub-Saharan Africa (11 kilograms). In rich countries, meat consumption per person is no longer increasing, but in the transitional countries of Asia and Latin America it still has considerable room to grow, and even more in the poor countries of Africa. According to one projection by the International Food Policy Research Institute, between 2010 and 2050 per capita meat consumption in Latin America is likely to rise by 33 percent, in East Asia and the Pacific by 86 percent, and in Sub-Saharan Africa by 118 percent (from a much lower level). Rich countries are the big meat consumers today, but in the decades ahead nearly all of the increase in meat consumption will take place in the developing world.

Most nutritionists endorse the consumption of some meat and dairy products (in addition to mother's milk, of course) as a source of beneficial micronutrients such as iron, zinc, calcium, and vitamins A and B12. Most of these same micronutrients are also available from plant sources, but in a form less easily taken up by the human body. Animal products can be particularly valuable for children going through a critical phase of accelerated physical growth and brain development in the first two years of life, and also for women with higher iron requirements in their reproductive years. At the same time, excessive consumption of meat and animal products is associated with a number of poor health outcomes, including a variety of cancers, heart diseases, and stroke. In urban China between 1982 and 2002, when meat and dairy products in the average diet increased from 11 percent by weight up to 25 percent, the prevalence of diabetes, hypertension, heart disease, and stroke all increased sharply as well.

Meat consumption per capita has finally leveled off in today's rich countries, and in the United States it has actually begun to decline, falling by 10 percent between 2004 and 2012. The reasons for this decline include the post-2007 economic recession, higher meat prices linked to higher animal feed costs (linked in turn to an increased use of corn for ethanol), growing health concerns within an aging generation of baby boomers, plus increased public awareness of the many environmental and animal welfare concerns linked to modern livestock production.

This recent decline in meat consumption in the United States includes little in the way of a shift toward purely vegetarian diets. Small segments of the American public have always maintained vegetarian diets by abstaining completely from meat consumption, including poultry and seafood (but usually not eggs and dairy products). Currently a bit more than 3 percent of Americans identify themselves as vegetarians of this kind, which is up from roughly 1 percent four decades ago. A smaller share of these individuals even opt to consume no animal products at all, maintaining what is called a "vegan" diet. Particularly among health-conscious or countercultural younger people, vegetarian and vegan diets gain favor. Film stars ranging from Brad Pitt to Woody Harrelson have made it known that they are vegetarians, and in 2010 former president Bill Clinton followed his daughter's lead and adopted a vegan diet (after getting two stents on top of quadruple bypass surgery), explaining that he wanted to live to be a grandfather.

Most of the recent reduction in meat consumption in the United States reflects neither strict vegetarianism or veganism, but simply an increased frequency of meatless meals or meals with less meat, particularly red meat. This trend has been promoted since 2003 by public health professionals through a Meatless Monday campaign, which in 2012 claimed to have a national participation rate of 18 percent. The original goal of the campaign was to cut saturated fat consumption in the United States by 15 percent, down to a USDA-recommended level. The only large nation in which full vegetarianism is widespread is India, where an estimated 31 percent of the population (mostly Hindus and Jains) are vegetarians. In Europe, vegetarians are most prevalent in Italy (10 percent of the population) and least prevalent in France (only 2 percent).

Is a vegetarian diet healthier?

Dietary health requires a balance of nutrients, and for most people meat is a convenient part of this balance, but it is not strictly necessary. The Mayo Clinic confirms that even for growing children and adolescents vegetarian diets can be safe and healthy. Getting protein is not a problem, since vegetarians who are not vegans can get animal protein from milk and eggs, and even vegans can get abundant protein from beans, legumes, and nuts. Calcium is not a problem for vegetarians who consume dairy products, and vegans can get calcium from green vegetables or from products fortified with calcium, such as soymilks, cereals, and juices. Vegans must take special care to get vitamins D and B12; the latter in particular may require seeking out fortified foods or supplements.

It can be more convenient to secure the needed balance of nutrients from a less restrictive non-vegetarian diet, but non-vegetarians can of course lapse into imbalances of other kinds. Non-vegetarian diets too often include inadequate helpings of fruits and vegetables, too much red meat, too many processed meats like bacon, sausage, and salami (containing risk-inducing nitrites as preservatives), and too many over-cooked charred meats that carry cancer risks. When it comes to health, what matters most about meat is the quantity consumed and the way in which it is processed or cooked, not the fact that it is meat. One 2005 study from the German Cancer Research Center compared health-conscious meat eaters to vegetarians and found no difference in mortality rates.

In some societies, purely vegetarian diets are simply not an option. On drylands in Africa where there is not enough water for vegetable crops, communities could not be sustained without cattle, sheep, and goats, which are ruminant animals with an extra stomach, allowing them to thrive on grasses that people cannot digest, converting those grasses into meat and milk for people. Likewise in arctic regions, human societies could not survive if they did not eat meat from fish and animals. Even in agricultural societies where producing vegetable food is an option, the sale of meat or milk from animals is often an essential income source for poor people who lack access to cropland.

If people in rich countries ate less meat, would hunger be reduced in poor countries?

Yes, but only by a small amount. If meat consumption declined, international meat and animal feed prices would also decline, but this would matter little for the vast proportion of hungry people, because they do not consume much that comes from the world market, and particularly not meat or animal feed. What these poor people need is more income to purchase rice, white maize, sorghum, millet, yams, cassava, or banana in their own local markets, not a lower international price for meat and feed. Most of the effects of lower meat consumption in rich countries would be confined to those same rich countries. Fewer cattle would be grazed on rangelands in Texas or Australia, but since these lands are too dry for growing crops, they would simply go unused. Less corn and soy would be produced for animal feed, and this would free up some more land for wheat and rice production, but the impact on international wheat and rice prices would be small.

The International Food Policy Research Institute has used a computer model of global agricultural markets to estimate the reduction in hunger that would result from a 50 percent reduction in per capita meat consumption in all high-income countries, from current levels. Under this extreme and unlikely assumption, there would be 700,000 fewer chronically malnourished children in the developing world by the year 2030, compared to a "business as usual" scenario. This is a measurable gain, but very small relative to the size of the problem. Under the "business as usual" scenario, there will be 134 million cases of child malnutrition in 2030, so the payoff from a 50 percent cut in meat consumption in rich countries is only a one-half of 1 percent reduction in child hunger. Reducing meat consumption in rich countries remains an excellent idea for the purpose of improving health and moderating environmental damage in those same rich countries, but not for getting more food to the hungry.

What are CAFOs?

Concentrated animal feeding operations, called CAFOs, are highly specialized industrial-scale facilities where large numbers of animals are kept in confinement for poultry, pork, beef, or dairy production. In wealthy countries, led by the United States, these systems have now largely replaced the small and diversified barnyard-style livestock systems that were once managed by individual farmers. CAFOs are a proven way to deliver higher volumes of standardized animal products to consumers at a much lower market price, yet they carry nonmarket costs and generate growing opposition from advocates for animal welfare, public health, and environmental protection.

CAFOs spread first to the poultry sector in the United States in the 1950s, then to the swine and cattle sector in the 1970s and 1980s. CAFOs are defined by the Environmental Protection Agency according to the number of animals they house. If an animal feeding operation has more than 700 mature dairy cattle, more than 1,000 cattle, or more than 30,000 laying hens or broiler chickens, it is considered a "large" CAFO and is automatically subject to regulation by the Environmental Protection Agency (EPA) under the Clean Water Act. CAFOs are spreading internationally and are now especially prevalent in China, Thailand, and Vietnam, where growth is driven by rapidly rising consumer demand for meat, poultry, and eggs. The United Nations Food and Agriculture Organization (FAO) has estimated that 80 percent of all growth in livestock production around the world now takes place within "industrial" CAFO-style systems.

Are CAFOs bad for animal welfare?

CAFOs manage farm animals under highly regulated conditions, typically in crowded confinement. Automated feed delivery and waste removal replace grazing and foraging, plus many of the traditional husbandry practices performed by human labor. This approach reduces land, labor, and facilities costs per unit of meat or milk produced, but even within the best maintained facilities, the impacts on animal welfare are problematic. The animals may face fewer risks from weather exposure and wild predators, and in some instances less harm from social conflict with each other, but they will be denied opportunities to engage in numerous instinctive behaviors—such as walking, perching, wing-flapping, or foraging—traditionally central to their daily routines. For example, in CAFOs pregnant sows weighing 400 pounds may be confined to iron "gestation crates" 7 feet long and 22 inches wide, in which they are unable to turn around. They will be on slatted floors that make cleanup easier, but this will leave them with no bedding and nothing to root around in.

In 2005, the American Veterinary Medical Association— which has close ties to the livestock industry—convened a task force to determine whether sows were harmed by confinement, and found that the research was mixed. This does not satisfy independent advocates for animal welfare who have no doubt that the CAFO model is harmful not only to sows in crates but also to egg-laying hens in small "battery" cages. The Humane Society of the United States (HSUS) and other activist groups, such as People for Ethical Treatment of Animals (PETA), are now waging campaigns to restrict or even eliminate the use of crates and cages.

Sometimes these campaigns take the form of state-by-state ballot issues placed before voters; one early HSUS victory was a 2002 ballot measure outlawing gestation crates in Florida, followed by a 2008 measure outlawing crates plus battery cages in California. Another tactic is to confront industry directly with damaging publicity, including graphic undercover videos of injured or suffering animals. In 2012, after the HSUS released an exposé on a confinement facility that supplied pigs to meat giant Tyson Foods, a cascade of private food and food service companies announced that they would no longer be buying pork from pigs confined in crates. By October 2012, more than 30 fast food companies and food retailers had made this same pledge. Earlier in 2011, the HSUS also negotiated an agreement with the United Egg Producers (UEP) to work together to push for federal legislation to regulate treatment of birds in U.S. table egg production.

In the United States, CAFOs are regulated for human health and safety and for environmental protection, but until recently there have been few laws governing the welfare of the animals themselves, beyond those that apply to humane transport and slaughter. The United States has laws to protect companion animal welfare (the Animal Welfare Act of 1966), but farm animals were excluded, and between 1985 and 1995, to make things worse, at least 18 states passed laws explicitly exempting agriculture from existing animal cruelty laws. Other countries have embraced higher standards. In 1991, the U.K. government required pig farmers to have their animals in pens rather than crates by 1999. Pig-producing nations in the European Union (EU) were told to have their sows in pens by 2013, and some countries like Germany went much farther, introducing in 2003 a requirement that pigs have access to sunlight, toys for amusement, and at least 20 seconds of personal contact with the farmer every day. Skeptics suspect such regulations will prove difficult to enforce.

When tighter regulations increase costs, they can risk creating sales opportunities for much less heavily regulated suppliers from places like Russia, China, and Latin America. In the United States, it costs about 27 percent more to raise pork crate-free and without the use of antibiotics or hormones for growth. Following the 1999 crate ban in the United Kingdom, the pig herd in that country declined by 40 percent. On the other hand, some animal welfare measures have proved easily affordable for consumers. When the McDonald's Corporation began insisting on larger cages for egg-laying hens, the resulting increase in cost to consumers was calculated at only about 1 penny per egg.

What else generates opposition to CAFOs?

Critics of CAFOs typically point to three concerns beyond animal welfare: microbial contamination in meat, excessive use of antibiotics, and pollution of water and air.

The microbial contamination issue centers on a charge, made in popular films such as *Food, Inc.*, that cattle fed on grain such as corn in feedlots, rather than raised exclusively on pasture, are more prone to grow a particularly dangerous strain of *E. coli* bacteria (O157:H7) in their digestive system, increasing the likelihood of meat contamination during slaughter and processing. Science does not support this claim. Grass-fed beef is certainly more nutritious than feed-lot beef, because it has less fat, more vitamin A and E, and more omega-3 fatty acids, but there is no convincing scientific evidence that it is any less prone to O157:H7. For example, one study published in *Applied & Environmental Microbiology* in 2009 concluded, "Our study found similar prevalences of *E. coli* O157:H7 in the feces of organically and naturally raised beef cattle [on grass], and our prevalence estimates for cattle from these types of production systems are similar to those reported previously for conventionally raised feedlot cattle."

A far more genuine concern is excessive use of antibiotics in CAFO environments. The livestock industry has routinely given animals antibiotics, such as penicillin, not only to protect them from disease in crowded environments, but simply to promote weight gain. Surprisingly, 80 percent of antibiotic sales in the United States go to chickens, pigs, and cattle. This is a risk because it can speed the emergence of antibiotic-resistant strains of human pathogens. The livestock industry claims that only one-third of the antibiotics it employs are used in human medicine, but little data have been shared on how specific drugs are administered, to which animals, and why. The FDA began monitoring the presence of antibiotic-resistant bacteria in retail meat in 1996, through a National Antimicrobial Resistance Monitoring System (NARMS). The most recent report, released in 2013, indicated that over the previous decade ampicillin resistance in retail chickens had increased from 17 percent to 40 percent.

As early as 1977, the FDA had announced that it would begin banning some agricultural uses of antibiotics, but industry-friendly congressional resolutions against such bans forced the agency to back off. In 2004, the American Public Health Association adopted resolutions to restrict the use of antibiotics in meat production, but no action was taken. By 2009, according to the FDA's own figures, farmers were giving healthy animals nearly 30 million pounds of antibiotics. In Europe, such practices had been banned since 1998.

Finally, in 2012, a federal district court judge in New York ordered the FDA to ban the use of low-dose penicillin and two forms of tetracycline for weight gain purposes. As a result, the FDA initiated a three-year phase-out of antibiotic use on livestock for growth promotion purposes, and phased in a requirement for veterinary oversight of antibiotic use.

Strong opposition to CAFOs also emerges on environmental grounds. Concentrating hundreds or even thousands of animals in a confined space creates a concentrated threat to local air and water quality from the urine and manure of the animals. The resulting environmental harms may include excess nutrients in water (particularly nitrogen and phosphorus), which in turn can contribute to low levels of dissolved oxygen, leading to fish kills. Decomposing organic matter can also contribute to toxic algal blooms. CAFO systems attempt to confine the animal waste within on-site "lagoons," to be recycled later in a safe and controlled manner, but lagoon leakage can introduce pathogens into local drinking water. The EPA calculates that states with high concentrations of CAFOs experience on average 20 to 30 serious water quality problems per year. Dust and odors can lead to worker illness and respiratory problems for those living downwind from CAFOs.

In the United States, CAFOs have been regulated since 1972 under the Clean Water Act as "point sources" of pollution. A permit program sets effluent limit guidelines, and the guidelines were revised in 2003 to require that all permitted CAFOs develop nutrient management plans, but then were revised again in 2008 to require permits only for those CAFOs planning to discharge waste, a major loophole since the most environmentally damaging discharges are usually unplanned. In 1995, an eight-acre hog-waste lagoon in North Carolina burst, spilling 25 million gallons of manure into the New River, killing about 10 million fish and closing 364,000 acres of coastal wetlands to shellfishing. Two years later, a new state law was passed placing a moratorium on new construction of hog farms with more than 250 animals. Then, when Hurricane

Floyd hit North Carolina in 1999, at least five more manure lagoons burst and approximately 47 lagoons were completely flooded.

Ponds and streams in rural America have always been polluted by animal waste, but usually in a widely dispersed pattern. Thanks to the growth of CAFOs, more than half of all hog production in the United States is now concentrated in just three states: Iowa, North Carolina, and Minnesota. This can generate a far more concentrated pollution risk for nearby communities.

How important are fish as a source of food?

Fish and fishery products can be a valuable source of both protein and essential micronutrients. Fish are central to the diet in many cultures, particularly in Asia. Globally, fish provide nearly half the earth's population with roughly 20 percent of their total intake of animal protein. Fish consumption is lowest in Africa, with only 9 kilograms per person per year. In the United States, per capita consumption is more than 20 kilograms per person. Two-thirds of all fish consumption takes place in Asia, where in Japan the average annual intake is 66 kilograms per capita. Japan also has the lowest prevalence of obesity in the developed world and the longest life expectancy.

Growth in global fish consumption has been high, averaging 3.2 percent annually over the past half century. Fish used for food can either be from inland freshwater or from ocean saltwater, and are either captured or farmed. People eat not only finfish but many other water species as well, including large quantities of crustaceans such as crab; mollusks such as clams, mussels, and squid; and various other aquatic animals such as sea urchins. Traditionally, most fish consumption has been satisfied through capture (popular author Paul Greenberg has labeled fish "the last wild food"), but now roughly half the global supply comes from fish farming, referred to as aquaculture. This human move toward domesticating fish is roughly at the same stage as our first efforts to domesticate crops and animals 10,000 years ago.

Are wild fisheries collapsing?

The total catch of marine fish peaked in 1996 at 86 million tons but then declined and has recently stabilized at roughly 80 million tons. The United Nations rates ocean fisheries as either underexploited, fully exploited, or overexploited, and since 1974, when the ratings system was created, the percentage of stocks being overexploited has increased from 10 percent to 30 percent. These overexploited fisheries are producing below their biological and ecological potential and are in serious need of improved management. An added 57 percent of stocks are close to their maximum sustainable production and have no room for expansion. In 2002, at a World Summit on Sustainable Development in South Africa, participating nations agreed on a "Johannesburg Plan" to restore overexploited stocks by 2015, but this has remained largely an empty letter. A United Nations Food and Agriculture (FAO) organization report in 2012 stated bluntly, "the state of marine fisheries is worsening." This damage to wild fisheries is a dangerous modification to a vast natural ecology, not just a threat to economic or food security.

The overexploitation of marine fisheries has technological, economic, and political origins. The technology for finding and catching fish has steadily improved. Log-Range Navigation (LORAN), Global Positioning Systems (GPS), and Geographic Information Systems (GIS) allow vessels to pinpoint the most productive fishing grounds, and recent refinements to sonar technology even allow fishers to more quickly find distinct species of fish. To locate swordfish and tuna, aircraft are deployed with infrared sensors that detect subtle changes in the surface temperature of the ocean. Airborne electronic image intensifiers also can be used to detect the light given off at night by some marine algae when disturbed by passing schools of fish.

The economic driver for overexploitation is global income growth, particularly in Asia. In China, where consumers for centuries have considered fish beneficial to the brain, income growth has fueled high demand. Between 1990 and 2009, per capita fish consumption in China increased at an average annual rate of 6 percent, reaching 32 kilograms. China's share of world fish production also grew from 7 percent to 35 percent between 1961 and 2010, and the government is now planning to expand its long-range fishing fleet by another 16 percent before the end of 2015.

The political drivers for overfishing are more subtle. National governments have come to recognize the importance of sustainable exploitation, and under the UN Convention on the Law of the Sea they terminated open access to coastal fisheries by claiming waters within 200 miles of their shores as an exclusive economic zone (EEZ). In these waters off the coast of the United States, stocks have been partly restored thanks to a 1996 law, the Magnuson-Stevens Fishery Conservation and Management Act, that set targets for rebuilding each species. As of 2013, 21 of 44 species had met the rebuilding target, and 7 others had made significant progress, increasing their populations by at least 25 percent.

Fish that migrate beyond an EEZ remain at serious risk of overexploitation. In the open ocean, restricting the catch requires international cooperation, and this has not yet been forthcoming. International concern for bluefin tuna stocks, which had declined by 75 percent, triggered a 2010 proposal to ban international trade in bluefin tuna under the Convention on International Trade in Endangered Species (CITES), but the measure was blocked by states with a strong commercial interest in the catch. Japan, which imports 80 percent of Atlantic bluefin, led the opposition, but more than 70 other countries opposed the trade ban as well. Trade bans on fish are potentially powerful instruments, since 38 percent of fishery production enters international commerce, with the European Union by itself taking 40 percent of all global imports, and with both the United States and Japan depending on imports for more than half of their domestic consumption.

Sustainable stocks management is also frustrated by fishing activities that are illegal, unreported, and unregulated, known as IUU. Many developing countries lack the physical or technical capacity to patrol their EEZ, and in some cases government officials in those countries are easily bribed into giving permits to those who overfish. Most regional fisheries are nominally governed by regional fishery bodies (RFBs), but these organizations depend too much on voluntary compliance by member governments, many of whom are unwilling or unable to exercise control. To supplement these RFBs, the United States and the European Union have been cooperating bilaterally since 2011, looking for better ways to keep IUU fish off the world market.

Is fish farming a solution?

Fish can be raised in tanks and ponds and, with the aid of cages or nets, even in oceans, lakes, and rivers. Fully "farmed" fish are those hatched from eggs within the aquaculture facility and confined for their entire life cycle, whereas "ranched" fish spend part of their lives in the wild. Some will be hatched and released, then caught when they return (like ranched salmon), while others will be caught in the wild as juveniles, then fed in confinement until they reach market weight (like ranched bluefin tuna).

The global aquaculture industry is growing rapidly, both in fresh and saltwater. In 2010, the total farm-gate value of food fish production from aquaculture was estimated at $119 billion. By volume, 89 percent of this production took place in Asia. China by itself provides 60 percent of global aquaculture production; the other major Asian producers include India, Vietnam, Indonesia, Bangladesh, and Thailand. Aquaculture production has either stagnated or contracted recently in Japan, the United States, and several European countries (with the exception of Norway, which farms Atlantic salmon in marine cages). Two-thirds of all aquaculture species are provided with feed, which has become a significant feature of the industry.

The rapid growth of aquaculture has relieved some commercial pressure on wild fisheries, but the industry nonetheless remains controversial, often because of unsolved technical problems. Disease outbreaks have affected farmed Atlantic salmon in Chile, oysters in Europe, and marine shrimp in Asia, South America, and Africa. In 2011, a disease outbreak nearly wiped out marine shrimp farming in Mozambique.

In other cases, interactions between farmed and wild species are a concern. Wild Atlantic salmon collapsed as a commercial fishery in the 1960s. It has been replaced now by highly affordable farmed Atlantic salmon, but the farmed fish are often grown along wild salmon migration routes, posing risks such as farm-born diseases and parasites and wastes that create a pollution problem. A larger concern for carnivorous fish such as salmon and tuna is the toll taken on wild forage fish, such as herring and sardines. It requires 5–15 pounds of wild fish to grow a single pound of Atlantic bluefin tuna in a net pen, and overharvesting forage fish could bring damage to multiple commercial species.

In the United States, the fish farming industry is politically weak compared to crop and livestock farming because it is new and non-traditional. There is no national heritage of fish farming, no established cabinet agency to support fish farming, and no tradition of property rights for fish farmers. In addition, there is often strong local opposition from environmentalists plus residential and recreational users of water resources. Similar political and institutional patterns are visible in much of Europe. For these reasons, the industry is likely to continue to expand most rapidly in the developing countries of Asia. American and European consumers will become increasingly dependent on imports of farmed fish from abroad.

11

AGRIBUSINESS, SUPERMARKETS, AND FAST FOOD

What does the word "agribusiness" mean?

The term "agribusiness" was coined in 1957 by two professors at the Harvard Business School, Ray Goldberg and John H. Davis, in recognition of an important change then taking place in the American agricultural sector. The "on-farm" part of America's agricultural economy was shrinking relative to input supply industries upstream (seed, farm chemical, and machinery suppliers) and also relative to food storage, transport, processing, manufacturing, packaging, marketing, and retail industries downstream. Since farms had become just one part of a longer and more industrialized food value chain, it made sense to begin referring to the chain as a single integrated entity: agribusiness.

The new term stuck, a *Journal of Agribusiness* was founded, and soon after, more than 100 institutions of higher education in the United States began offering formal degrees in agribusiness. In 1990, the International Food and Agribusiness Management Association (IAMA) was founded as a worldwide networking organization and a bridge among multinational

agribusiness companies, researchers, educators, and government officials.

Why is agribusiness controversial?

For those inside most food and farm industries, the word
"agribusiness" is used as a descriptive term with no bad connotations; in fact, it even carries a flattering connotation of
modernity. Yet for critics from outside the sector, the term carries strongly negative connotations. It is deployed to suggest
that traditional and trustworthy family farmers have been
replaced by powerful profit-driven corporations not accountable for the damage they do to rural communities, human
health, and the environment.

Critiques of American agribusiness date from 1973, when a
Texas populist named Jim Hightower published a book titled
Hard Tomatoes, Hard Times. Hightower argued that corporate
power now dominated the U.S. Department of Agriculture
and even the nation's agricultural universities, leading to a
more rapid demise of small farms, displacing farmworkers
and bringing us unhealthy food. Agribusiness firms were also
a target of journalist Eric Schlosser's widely popular 1999 book
Fast Food Nation: The Dark Side of the All-American Meal. More
recently, in 2009, a popular film titled *Food, Inc.* asserted that
"our nation's food supply is now controlled by a handful of
corporations that often put profit ahead of consumer health,
the livelihood of the American farmer, the safety of workers
and our own environment."

These critics identify specific corporate villains along every
separate link in the value chain. Chemical companies and
multinational seed companies currently tend to attract the
greatest criticism, and because the St. Louis–based Monsanto
Company is both a chemical company (selling herbicides)
and a multinational biotechnology company (developing and
patenting genetically engineered crop seeds), it is frequently
the most vilified of all. Downstream from farms, among firms

that ship and handle farm commodities, a large company from Minneapolis named Cargill is frequently criticized, both for its secrecy as a privately held firm and for its alleged market power. Within the meat sector, Tyson Foods, Inc., of Springdale, Arkansas, the world's largest processor and marketer of chicken, beef, and pork, is depicted as an enemy of small family farmers and a threat to the environment. In the packaged food sector, ConAgra Foods, Inc., of Omaha, Nebraska, is said to damage consumer health by marketing heavily processed and chemical-laden foods such as frozen dinners, Slim Jims, and Reddi-wip. Finally, at the retail and food service end, McDonald's and Burger King are accused of addicting children to unhealthy burgers, fries, and sweetened drinks. In 2012, restaurants delivered $600 billion worth of meals and service, more than the total value of all U.S. farm sales, suggesting that the American economy now generates more money serving food than it does in growing food.

Food industries have long been an inviting target for populist attack. In 1906, a muckraking novel by Upton Sinclair, titled *The Jungle*, exposed disgraceful working conditions in Chicago's meatpacking industry. Like many critics of agribusiness today, Sinclair was motivated by a suspicion toward all private corporations, and he used the emotive issue of food to dramatize these larger suspicions. The book caused a sensation, but most readers skipped over the labor rights message and focused instead on a worry that industrial meat products might not be safe to eat. Sinclair's book led directly to passage of the Meat Inspection Act and the Pure Food and Drug Act of 1906 and to the creation of a national Food and Drug Administration (FDA).

Do agribusiness firms control farmers?

Farmers in America have always worried about the market power of non-farmers. Historically, they worried most about bankers, railroads, and grain traders; today, they worry most about concentration in the seed industry and in the meatpacking industry, where the market power of private companies vis-à-vis farmers has recently increased.

A fear of industry concentration in the international seed sector has arisen since the 1990s, following a proliferation of patent claims on genetically engineered seeds, accompanied by a rush of corporate mergers and acquisitions. Between 1985 and 2009, annual sales in global seed markets increased from $18 billion to about $44 billion. By 2008, the Monsanto Company and its subsidiaries owned more than 400 separate plant technology patents and claimed more than 20 percent of the global proprietary seed market. The top five companies had 54 percent.

On the other hand, this kind of concentration has limited reach because most countries around the world still do not allow seeds to be patented, and the vast majority do not even allow genetically engineered seeds to be planted. In addition, seed markets themselves provide only one part of the world's total seed supply. Many farmers in poor countries, and quite a few in rich countries as well, do not buy any seeds at all on a regular basis, instead planting seeds saved from their own harvest.

Within the seed markets that are proprietary, corporate concentration can be highly significant for some crops. For example, 96 percent of all genetically engineered cotton planted in the United States contains Monsanto's patented traits, and roughly 90 percent of all patented soybean traits are owned by Monsanto. Monsanto's first Roundup Ready soybean patent will expire in 2014, however—a reminder that the monopoly position provided by patents is always temporary. Companies enforce their seed patent claims in part through contracts with farmers called stewardship agreements, where farmers agree not to save and replant the seeds after harvest. The companies are also willing to go to court. According to one tally done by the Center for Food Safety in 2013, Monsanto has filed more than 140 patent infringement lawsuits over the years and has collected a total of $24 million in recorded judgments.

This does represent a new element of corporate control over farmers, but economic studies of the corn and cotton-seed industries show that the patented seeds have brought cost-reducing benefits that significantly outweigh any disadvantage posed by the patent claims or greater corporate concentration. Farmers buy these seeds because the traits help them cut production costs significantly. When patent-owning companies set their prices too high, as with Monsanto's bungled introduction of a new SmartStax corn variety in 2010, farmers balk and start buying seed from another company (in this case, from an Iowa-based rival, DuPont Pioneer). In 2009, DuPont Pioneer had pressed the Obama administration to initiate antitrust action against Monsanto, but a multiyear Justice Department investigation into Monsanto was closed in 2012, without any action taken.

Market concentration in the seed sector is to some extent an artifact of the stigmatizing political attacks leveled against genetically engineered seeds (discussed in Chapter 13). Such attacks dried up European investments in this technology, leaving U.S. companies like Monsanto with few international competitors. Inside the United States, in addition, government research money could have been used to develop this technology in the public sector without patent restrictions, but Congress cut back on such funding, which gave the private sector greater dominance.

The American meatpacking sector has also become highly concentrated in recent years. By 2005, four companies controlled the processing of more than 80 percent of the country's beef; three of those same four companies, along with an additional fourth, processed over 60 percent of the country's pork. Four major companies in broiler chicken processing (including Tyson Foods) now provide more than half of the country's chicken supply. Companies such as Tyson Foods work with thousands of individual "contract chicken growers" who provide their own land and construct their own sheds to raise the chickens, while the company owns the chickens and provides all the feed.

The growers who work for agribusiness firms under this sort of contract, as well as those still struggling to survive as independents, have reason to fear that the companies will use their market power to gain a disproportionate advantage. In the 1990s, America's hog slaughter industry also moved toward greater vertical integration and concentration, a move that left even the remaining independent producers with less market control. The next worrisome step in vertical integration might take place in cattle markets. A legislative measure to bar meatpackers from owning, feeding, or controlling cattle was inserted into the Senate-passed version of the 2008 farm bill but then was dropped in conference before the bill was passed.

Outside the biotech seed sector and the livestock sector, corporations do not yet have significant market power over farmers. The largest portion of all basic crop production in the United States now comes from very large farms, but most are still family corporations (with more than half of the voting stock held by family members). Non-family corporations account for only 6 percent of all farm sales. As for control from downstream crop purchasing companies, competitive markets tend to prevail here as well, in part because concentration among the purchasing companies is offset by the countervailing power of farmer marketing cooperatives, which can be formed legally under America's federal marketing order system.

It is a stretch to imagine, as some do, that international corporations control the lives of poor farmers in the developing world. Most poor farmers in Africa do not make any purchases of seeds at all (they save seeds from the previous season's crop), and they make only minimal purchases of fertilizers and pesticides. When they do market a portion of their crop, it is usually to local buyers or to government-regulated marketing boards, rather than to vertically integrated agribusiness firms. Private international companies are not interested in most African farmers because they lack the purchasing power to be good customers. In Africa, only 2 percent of all investment in agricultural research comes from private firms. The danger is less that international investors will control poor farmers in Africa, and more that they will continue to ignore them.

Do food companies and supermarkets control consumers?

Critics suspect that agribusiness firms, including retail supermarket chains, exploit their market power to raise the cost of food to consumers. When food prices rose sharply in the United States in the 1970s, Jim Hightower (of *Hard Tomatoes* fame) alleged that without the monopoly power of agribusiness, food would have been 25 percent cheaper for the American consumer. Careful studies by economists show that monopoly power in the food manufacturing industry does raise costs to consumers, but not by a large percentage. Bruce Gardner, a leading American agricultural economist, calculated that in the 1990s only about 2 percent of the consumer's final marketing bill went to pay for "excess profits" due to imperfect market competition.

With respect to supermarkets, studies show that the industry has become more concentrated, and in cities with fewer competing stores, consumer food prices are indeed higher. Yet the rate of profit in the retail food industry overall, measured per dollar of sales, has not increased over time, thanks to the efficiencies from larger store size that are passed on to consumers. A study by the U.S. Department of Agriculture's Economic Research Service in 1989 found no significant effect on supermarket prices from increasing industry concentration. A review by the Federal Trade Commission in 1990 found the same. Instead of controlling consumers, modern supermarkets compete with each other to attract customers by offering an ever growing array of affordable food purchase options.

Some food companies have clearly held near-monopoly positions for individual food products. For example, General Foods has enjoyed nearly 90 percent of the market in Jell-O-like products. Yet there is no convincing evidence that the company's profits from Jell-O have been higher than for products such as peanut butter, where there is much more competition. If profits begin to move up, competitors will move in, as in the case of the creatively blended ice cream sold by Ben & Jerry's, which became so successful that it quickly inspired competing alternative brands. The American food industry has roughly 300,000 individual firms overall, more than enough to provide competition. In the 1970s, the Federal Trade Commission looked at charges that the three largest breakfast cereal companies (Kellogg's, General Foods, and General Mills, which together had 80 percent of the market) were engaged in predatory behavior by proliferating their own brands to monopolize store shelf space. But, after a 10-year investigation, the case was dropped. In subsequent years, the market share of these top three companies fell in any case, as new private-label companies moved into the sector.

Are supermarkets spreading into developing countries?

Supermarkets are pervasive in rich countries, and they now are spreading rapidly into the developing world, bringing more choices for consumers but uncertain consequences for competing retailers and local food producers.

Supermarkets tend to spring up naturally wherever people have increased incomes and refrigerators, wherever women have entered the workforce, and wherever automobile ownership has begun to spread. North America, Europe, and Japan have fit this profile for decades. In France today, just as in the United States, 70–80 percent of national food retail sales are made in supermarkets. More surprising has been the recent and rapid spread of supermarkets into parts of the developing world where affluence, auto ownership, and female workforce participation are not yet as fully developed.

In Latin America, only 10 percent of all food retail sales were made through supermarkets as recently as the 1980s, but by 2000, that figure rose to 50–60 percent. Supermarkets took off five to seven years later in East Asia and Southeast Asia and then exhibited even faster growth. In Taiwan and South Korea, supermarket sales quickly gained a 63 percent share of all food sales. In China, as recently as 1991, there were no supermarkets at all, yet by 2001, the supermarket share in Chinese urban food markets was 48 percent. Supermarkets do not yet serve as many customers in South Asia or in Sub-Saharan Africa. For example, retail market shares in India and in Nigeria have recently reached only 5 percent.

One key factor in the spread of supermarkets in poor countries has been electrification and the availability of home refrigerators, which make possible the purchase of fresh foods in larger quantity on a less frequent basis. Second has been the opening of more national economies in the developing world to foreign direct investment, particularly since the 1990s. This gave established supermarket chains, such as Ahold, Carrefour, Tesco, and Wal-Mart, opportunities to move quickly into the retail food markets of Latin America and Asia. Three of every ten pesos spent on food in Mexico today is spent at a Wal-Mart.

Local consumers generally benefit when supermarkets arrive, because they gain access to a wider variety of food purchase options offered at a higher standard for both food safety and cosmetic appearance, and usually at a lower cost. Some local farmers and local food wholesale and retail competitors will be threatened, however.

Traditional local farmers usually cannot provide the steady supply of top-quality fresh food that a multinational supermarket will require, because of inferior harvest techniques and lack of post-harvest product protection, resulting in lower-quality produce. As a consequence, traditional local farmers tend to be bypassed by supermarket buyers, who purchase instead from modern-style specialty farms, often created through still more foreign investment. These farms deliver contracted produce either to the supermarket directly or, more likely, to yet another new commercial institution, a distribution center that will serve as supplier to multiple local supermarkets. Systems of this kind bypass both traditional local farms and traditional urban wholesale markets. The rapid insertion of these exotic systems into food markets in the developing world changes the diet of consumers (encouraging the consumption of more packaged foods, processed foods, and internationally branded imported foods) and it also changes the market position of local food producers and wholesalers, keeping them away from the most affluent local customer base.

Is Wal-Mart taking over food retailing in Africa and India?

Wal-Mart is the world's largest retailer (of much more than just food). It is the largest private employer in the world, with 10,000 stores in 27 different countries, under nearly 70 different names. Wal-Mart's data-mining capacity is second only to that of the Pentagon. Until recently, supermarkets like Wal-Mart had a relatively small footprint both in Africa (where income growth is still lagging) and in India (mostly because the government of India did not allow foreign retailers majority ownership in "multi-brand" stores). Then, in 2011, Wal-Mart decided to invest in Africa, purchasing for $2.4 billion a majority share in the South African retail chain Massmart, which operated 290 stores in 13 African countries. Wal-Mart had earlier lost out in Asia to fast-moving rivals like Tesco and did not want this to happen in Africa.

Gaining access to the Indian market remained more difficult. In 2011 the Indian Cabinet approved a plan to permit foreign retailers majority ownership, but then pulled back for a year in the face of strong opposition from small traders and shopkeepers who feared they would be put out of business. But when India's economic growth began slowing in 2012, the government revived its plan to attract more foreign investment into the retail sector, and the president of Wal-Mart's Indian unit responded by promising to come in as a good citizen, investing to help build the infrastructure that India needs to lower retail costs and reduce post-harvest waste. Critics and opposition party leaders knew that Wal-Mart was being investigated for earlier paying millions of dollars in bribes to local officials in Mexico when it expanded its operations there, and they warned that the same aggressive approach would be used to corrupt officials in India. Paying bribes ("speed money") to local officials is often the only way to make things happen in India, where in some states retail chains must secure 50 to 60 separate regulatory approvals before they can open a store. But an international investor like Wal-Mart will come under a higher level of scrutiny if it follows this path.

Are fast food restaurant chains spreading unhealthy eating habits worldwide?

Unhealthy eating styles are spreading globally. According to one 2012 estimate, three decades from now, if current trends continue, people in today's low- and middle-income countries will be consuming as much unhealthy food as people today in rich countries. Increased consumption of packaged foods, snack foods, and soft drinks purchased from supermarkets will be part of this trend, but increased patronage at fast food ("quick-service") restaurant chains will contribute as well.

Quick-service chains went global in the 1980s and 1990s, moving into many countries alongside supermarkets and at an equally rapid rate. In 1990, South Korea had four McDonald's restaurants; five years later, it had 48. In the same short five-year period, China went from having one McDonald's restaurant to 62. Indonesia went from none to 38. Brazil went from 63 to 243. During this high-growth period, a new McDonald's restaurant was opening somewhere in the world every three hours. Critics see this as an unfortunate imposition of bad food—as well as America's most garish commercial culture—onto new urbanites in the developing world, who are naively enthralled at becoming more "Western."

As usual, the picture is more complicated. Quick-service "street food" for urbanites pre-dated the arrival of McDonald's restaurants. In Asia, takeaway stands selling salty fried foods have long been a not-so-healthy option. In South Asia, street foods abound, for example *panipuri*, which is fried bread with a spice and potato filling. In the Middle East, flatbread and falafel to go are found everywhere. In urban West Africa, ready-to-eat char-grilled meat sticks have long been popular. To some extent, Western fast foods are merely a replacement for these traditional local fast foods, many of which also fall short of providing a balanced diet.

On the issue of cultural imperialism, anthropologists who study the impact of fast food restaurants in developing countries have found a mixed result. In many East Asian settings, fast food restaurants do not replace traditional cuisine because they are often a place to go for a snack between meals, or to socialize with friends after school. Asian customers view fast food chains as distinctly modern but not always foreign. In China, McDonald's restaurants are 50 percent Chinese owned, nearly all are Chinese managed, and 95 percent of the food sold is sourced from China. Surveys reveal that a majority of the young customers even believe that Ronald McDonald is Chinese and lives in Beijing. Instead of changing China's family-oriented food culture, McDonald's makes money by catering to it. Entire families are welcomed for parties and celebrations, with paper and pen provided for young children to write and draw. Teahouses and art galleries are common features as well. Customers were initially attracted to fast food restaurants in China because they had clean toilets, a benefit that competing local restaurants soon had to provide as well.

The chains that do best are those that follow local dietary preferences. KFC outsells McDonald's in China because chicken is more of a staple in the traditional Chinese diet than beef. Subway offers kosher food in Israel, nearly all of their restaurants in Muslim countries are *halal*, and beef-free, pork-free, and vegetarian products are offered in India. McDonald's has also enjoyed rapid growth in India, with 250 restaurants in 2011 and plans to double that number by 2014. In Hindu India, where cows are revered, beef has been taken off the menu and replaced by vegetable patties and giant Maharaja Macs made with chicken.

In countries such as China and India, it is the rise of an urban middle class that has done the most to alter traditional eating practices. Multinational supermarkets and fast food chains expand to make money as soon as this underlying shift begins, and they even speed it along and shape it in a Western direction, but urbanization and income growth would have changed eating patterns in these countries even without supermarkets or Western fast food.

12

ORGANIC AND LOCAL FOOD

What is organic food?

The label "organic" refers to a method of food production. Organic food is produced without any human-made (i.e., synthetic) fertilizers, pesticides, or preservatives. In organic systems, farmers use a variety of methods that do not require synthetic substances. For example, soil fertility is maintained by planting legumes that fix nitrogen naturally, or by using animal-derived nutrients such as composted manure. Insects are controlled using biological methods (relying on birds or spiders that eat insect pests), or by using naturally occurring pesticides such as Bt (a soil bacterium) or pyrethrins (produced by chrysanthemums) or sabadilla (derived from the ground seeds of lilies). Weeds are controlled not with synthetic herbicides but with mechanical cultivation or mulching. In place of synthetic preservatives, organic foods are traditionally cured with salt.

Prior to the development of synthetic nitrogen fertilizers in the early twentieth century, all food production world-wide was de facto organic. Only in the twentieth century did organic methods come to be classified as distinct from emerging modern methods and then given a distinct label (the original label was "biodynamic"). Organically grown foods are not to be confused with foods sold as "natural," which are minimally processed foods that also do not contain manufactured ingredients such as refined sugar, food colorings, or flavorings. Foods can be natural but not organic, just as they can be organic but not natural.

What is the history of organic food?

The organic food movement began in Europe early in the twentieth century, originally as a philosophical rejection of synthetic nitrogen fertilizer. In 1909, two German chemists, Fritz Haber and Carl Bosch, had discovered a method to capture atmospheric nitrogen for agricultural use by combining it with hydrogen under high temperature and pressure, resulting in ammonia. Followers of a pre-scientific "vitalist" philosophy, who asserted that living things such as plants could only be properly nurtured by the products of other living things (e.g., other plants, or animal manure), rejected this method of capturing nitrogen. The strongest rejection came in Austria, where the philosopher Rudolf Steiner championed what he called biodynamic ("life force") farming, which meant growing crops with composted animal manure plus other preparations such as chamomile blossom and oak bark. Steiner's approach was later promoted in Germany under the Third Reich by Rudolf Hess and Heinrich Himmler, who had come to doubt the sustainability of using artificial fertilizer and advocated instead "agriculture in accordance with the laws of life."

Skepticism toward synthetic nitrogen fertilizer was also found in England at the time, where elements of the aristocracy (including Sir Albert Howard and Lady Eve Balfour) took the lead in arguing against what they considered "artificial manures." To the present day, organic farming has strong support within the English upper class, most notably from Prince Charles, who in 1986 converted his own Duchy Home Farm to a completely organic system.

The term "organic farming" was not coined until 1942, when the American Jerome Irving (J. I.) Rodale, who had taken inspiration from Sir Albert Howard's writings, began publishing a magazine he titled *Organic Gardening and Farming*. Rodale was also a promoter of alternative health care methods, and in the 1950s he founded *Prevention* magazine.

Organic backyard gardening has always been popular, but organic commercial farming was not at first promoted, in part because production costs were high and the demand for organic products was low. Organic products cost 10 to 40 percent more than conventionally grown products, and they were at first sold only in specialty markets or health stores. The organic option gained a stronger popular following after Rachel Carson's compelling critique of synthetic pesticide use in her 1962 book, *Silent Spring*. A movement that began as a rejection of synthetic fertilizer thus was reenergized by Carson's rejection of synthetic pesticides.

Organic advocacy from both growers and consumers eventually led Congress, in 1990, to mandate the creation of a clear national standard for certifying and labeling organically grown products. The emergence of this credible certification and labeling standard triggered a far more rapid expansion of both organic production and sales. Because organically grown foods commanded a higher price in the marketplace, even growers not attracted to the movement on philosophical grounds could find a commercial incentive to convert to organic production systems.

How is organic food regulated in the United States?

Organic foods are regulated under a National Organic Program (NOP) created in 2002 by the U.S. Department of Agriculture (USDA). Under this program, foods can be labeled "organic" only if grown and handled by certified organic producers and processors. The certification is performed not by the USDA directly but by third-party government-accredited certifiers who charge a fee. Certification can cost approximately $700 per farm in the first year, then $400 annually in later years.

Certification is based on a requirement that only "non-synthetic" substances be used in organic production and handling. Synthetic fertilizers and pesticides are generally prohibited, along with the use of sewage sludge for fertilizer, the use of irradiation to kill food pathogens, and the planting of genetically engineered seeds. The USDA's original proposal would have allowed the use of sewage sludge, irradiation, and genetically engineered seeds, but outraged advocates for organic food sent 275,000 letters of complaint, so the government agreed in the end to exclude all three. Farms must be free of all prohibited substances and practices for at least three years to qualify for certification. In animal production, any animals used for meat, milk, or eggs must be fed 100 percent organic feed, have access to the outdoors, and may not be given hormones or antibiotics. Certified handlers of food must use only organic ingredients and must prevent organic and non-organic products from coming into contact with each other. The products marketed by certified growers and handlers are entitled to carry a prominent logo that says "USDA Organic."

Once this system began operating in 2002, consumer confidence in the integrity of organic sellers increased, and commercial sales began increasing rapidly at annual rates originally above 15 percent, slowing to 7 percent by 2010. The organic sector nonetheless remains small in the United States, making up only 4 percent of total food purchases as of 2010. Organically grown foods are produced on only one-half of 1 percent of harvested cropland in the United States.

Is most organic food grown on small farms?

Most of the individual farms in the organic sector are still small and highly diversified, but the bulk of organic production does not come from these small farms. Small farms with less than $100,000 in annual sales represent 70 percent of all individual organic farms in America, but together they make only 7 percent of all sales. Operations of any size can seek organic certification, so most commercial production now comes from large and highly specialized organic farms. For example, in 2011, half of all organic crops grown in the United States came from just one state—California—and three-quarters of all production came from large farms with annual sales of more than $1 million. Earthbound Farm in California operates 37,000 acres, growing organic packaged salads and baby greens. Most organic milk production also comes from large farms. Before pasture requirements were clarified in 2010, organic certification was permitted for massive industrial operations that milked as many as 10,000 cows.

Large numbers of small organic farmers still sell their products through local farmers' markets, but this is now just a small part of total organic sales. As early as 2002, only 13 percent of organic vegetable sales were still being made through farmers' markets; most of the rest was moving through supermarkets like Wal-Mart. A growing share of organic food on the market is now also being sold in packaged and processed form, by large food companies such as PepsiCo, Kellogg, or Kraft. Despite this commercial expansion, organically grown foods have remained considerably more expensive than their conventional counterparts. One 2011 survey of offerings at Safeway revealed that organic strawberries, broccoli, milk, and eggs cost 19 percent, 58 percent, 66 percent, and 128 percent more than the conventional alternatives.

Philosophical advocates for organic farming fight against the industrial aspects of modern organic production, fearing that the big growers will lobby the USDA to weaken the organic standard for their own convenience. When the big growers and food companies moved in, for example, they managed to secure a 2006 amendment to the organic standard that created a list of "synthetic substances allowed for use" in certified organic crop production. This weakening of the standard took place over objections from purists such as the Cornucopia Institute and the Organic Consumers Association (OCA).

Is organic food more nutritious and safe?

Consumers who pay more to purchase organic foods do so for multiple reasons. With organic fruits and vegetables, the motivation is often to gain a nutritional advantage, or to avoid pesticide residues on food, or to increase farmworker safety and protect the environment. Purchasers of organic meats and other livestock products often want to avoid microbial contamination, excessive antibiotic use, and the confined treatment of animals that typifies conventional livestock operations.

Strictly on nutritional grounds, health professionals from outside the organic community have found little or no advantage from organic foods. Claims of superior nutrient content continue to be made by the Organic Center, an institution founded in 2002 to demonstrate the benefits of organic products. For example in 2008, the Organic Center published a review "confirming" the nutrient superiority of plant-based organic foods, showing that they contained more vitamin C and vitamin E and a higher concentration of polyphenols, such as flavonoids. This review was rebutted, however, by conventional nutritionists who explained that the Organic Center had used statistical results that were either not peer reviewed or not significant in terms of human health. Organic milk from cows raised on grass may indeed contain 50 percent more beta-carotene, but there is so little beta-carotene in milk to begin with that the resulting gain is only an extra 112 micrograms of beta-carotene per quart of milk, or less than 1 percent the quantity of beta-carotene found in a single medium-size baked sweet potato.

According to the Mayo Clinic, "No conclusive evidence shows that organic food is more nutritious than is conventionally grown food." European health professionals tend to agree. Claire Williamson from the British Nutrition Foundation states, "From a nutritional perspective, there is currently not enough evidence to recommend organic foods over conventionally produced foods." In 2009, the *American Journal of Clinical Nutrition* published a study, commissioned by the British Food

Standards Agency, of 162 scientific papers produced in the past 50 years on the health and diet benefits of organically grown foods and found no evidence of a benefit. The director of the study concluded, "Our review indicates that there is currently no evidence to support the selection of organically over conventionally-produced on the basis of nutritional superiority." In 2012, a review of data from 237 studies conducted through the Center for Health Policy at Stanford University, published in the *Annals of Internal Medicine,* concluded that there were no convincing differences between organic and conventional foods in nutrient content or health benefits.

The claim that organic food is safer due to lower pesticide residues is also suspect in the eyes of most health professionals. The Mayo Clinic says, "Some people buy organic food to limit their exposure to [pesticide] residues. Most experts agree, however, that the amount of pesticides found on fruits and vegetables poses a very small health risk." Residues on food can be a significant problem in developing countries, where the spraying of pesticides is poorly regulated and where fruits and vegetables are often sold unwashed, straight from the field. Yet in advanced industrial countries such as the United States, foods sold through commercial channels have residue levels that present only the smallest risk to health. In 2003, the Food and Drug Administration (FDA) analyzed several thousand samples of domestic and imported foods in the U.S. marketplace and found that only 0.4 percent of the domestic samples and only 0.5 percent of the imported samples had detectable chemical residues that exceeded the regulatory tolerance levels set by the United Nations through the Food and Agriculture Organization (FAO) and the World Health Organization (WHO).

These tolerance levels intentionally err on the side of caution. The UN establishes acceptable daily intake (ADI) levels for each separate pesticide, set conservatively at 1/100th of an exposure that still does not cause toxicity in laboratory animals. Actual exposure levels, in turn, are almost always far below the ADI level. When the FDA surveyed the highest exposures to 38 chemicals in the diets of various population subgroups in the United States, it found that for 4 of these 38 chemicals, the highest exposures were still less than 5 percent of the ADI level. For the other 34 chemicals, exposures were even lower, less than 1 percent of the ADI level. Carl K. Winter and Sarah F. Davis, food scientists at the University of California–Davis and the Institute of Food Technologies, conclude from these data, "[T]he marginal benefits of reducing human exposure to pesticides in the diet through increased consumption of organic produce appear to be insignificant."

It is true that conventional foods are sometimes not safe to consume, but organically grown foods can also carry risks. In 2006, bagged fresh spinach from a California farm in its final year of converting to organic certification was the source of E. coli infections in the United States that killed at least three and sickened hundreds. In 2009, there were nine documented fatal episodes of salmonella poisoning from peanut butter and ground peanut products traced to peanut plants in Texas and Georgia, both of which had organic certification. In 2011, 53 people died from eating bean sprouts that were organically grown in Germany yet were contaminated with E. coli bacteria.

Is organic farming better for the environment?

Organic farming systems are in some ways better for protecting the natural environment but in other ways they may be worse. As a general rule, organic systems are less likely to generate damaging chemical runoff and groundwater pollution, yet they will require the clearing of more land per bushel of production, which makes them a threat—if scaled up—to forests, fragile lands, and wildlife habitat.

Organic food is often promoted as friendly to the environment because there is no synthetic fertilizer or pesticide use. This is correct, yet the assertion must be qualified because organic farmers who over-apply or mismanage animal waste can also pollute groundwater and surface water. Conversely, well-managed conventional systems, through the employment of no-till practices and precision applications of water and chemicals, can keep environmental damage to a minimum.

The best farming systems for the environment will actually integrate conventional and organic methods. For example, soil health is often best protected when prudent quantities of synthetic chemical fertilizers are used in combination with cover crops, crop rotations, and manure. Yet this best practice is blocked by the rigid organic standard, because the use of any synthetic nitrogen is strictly prohibited. Pest control is best accomplished through integrated pest management (IPM) methods that begin with natural biological controls but allow careful applications of chemical insecticides as a last resort, yet even the smallest use of synthetic chemicals is blocked under the organic standard. The strict prohibition against synthetic herbicide use in organic farming also holds back the use of no-till practices, which are a superior method for avoiding soil erosion, burning less diesel fuel, and reducing greenhouse gas emissions. The organic standard also makes it impossible to plant genetically engineered crops such as Bt corn and Bt cotton, which help conventional farmers reduce insecticide use. Environmental protection was not the original motive for advocating organic methods a century ago, so these environmental limitations embedded in the organic standard today should not be surprising.

The much larger land requirements of organic systems are the biggest environmental risk that they carry. In the United States, according to USDA surveys of actual farms, yields per acre for organic row crops and vegetables are found to be only 40–80 percent as high as the conventional average. This means that organic farms must plant more land to secure each bushel of production. The same is true in Europe, where organically grown cereal crops have yields only 60–70 percent as high as those conventionally grown. In the United Kingdom, organic winter wheat yields are only 4 tons per hectare compared to

8 tons per hectare for conventional farms. If Europe tried to feed itself organically, it would need an additional 28 million hectares of cropland, equal to all the remaining forest cover of France, Germany, Denmark, and Britain combined.

The uncertain environmental payoff from organic farming was confirmed in a 2012 report by scientists at Oxford University, published in the *Journal of Environmental Management*. Based on findings from 71 peer-reviewed studies, this report concluded that organic systems were often better for the environment per unit of land, but conventional systems were often better per unit of production. In other words, as production requirements increase, the environmental cost of holding to the organic standard will increase as well. In terms of greenhouse gas emissions, this Oxford study also found that organic milk, cereals, and pork production generated higher greenhouse gas emissions per unit of output than the conventional alternative.

Could today's world be fed with organically grown food?

Assuming current levels of consumption, it is no longer possible to feed the world with organic farming systems that prohibit the use of synthetic nitrogen fertilizer. In the past century, the population of the earth has increased from 1.6 billion to 7 billion, and these much larger numbers are being fed thanks largely to higher crop yields made possible by synthetic nitrogen. Since the 1930s, for example, wheat yields in conventional farming using nitrogen fertilizer have doubled. Vaclav Smil, an agronomist from the University of Manitoba, calculates that synthetic fertilizers currently supply about 40 percent of all the nitrogen used by crops around the world. To replace this synthetic nitrogen with organic nitrogen would require the manure production of approximately 7–8 billion additional cattle, roughly a fivefold increase from current numbers, creating an unacceptable environmental burden. Feeding of all these animals organically, without crops grown using nitrogen fertilizer, would require a conversion of much of the earth's surface to pasture land, an intolerable option on both economic and environmental grounds.

Advocates for organic farming, such as the International Federation of Organic Agricultural Movements (IFOAM), do not address the problem in such terms. They assert that organic practices can increase yields, based on farming projects they have carried out in some of the world's hungriest regions, such as Africa. They point for documentation to a 2006 meta-study in the journal *Renewable Agriculture and Food Systems* and to a 2008 United Nations report titled *Organic Agriculture and Food Security in Africa*. Yet most of the yield claims made in these studies are based on project-level comparisons between improved organic systems and traditional systems that provide no soil improvements at all, rather than on comparisons between organic and conventionally fertilized "green revolution" systems.

Many of Africa's smallholder farmers today are actually de facto organic, because they use no synthetic fertilizers or pesticides, and they are not more productive as a result. Certified organic farming has expanded in Africa in recent years, but mostly to grow crops for export to supermarkets in Europe, rather than to provide food for local consumption.

What is the local food movement?

When industrial-scale operations began taking over organic farming in the United States, advocates looking for alternatives began to demand something more: local food, purchased directly from growers at farmers' markets, community gardens, co-ops, or through community-supported agriculture (CSA) subscriptions.

The social movement to promote locally grown food was consolidated in the United States in 2005, when Jessica Prentice, the founder of a community-supported kitchen in Berkeley, California, coined the term "locavore" to describe those who opt to get their food, when possible, from within a 100-mile radius (the 100-mile diet). It became clear that significant numbers of consumers were willing to pay more for locally grown food, so farmers' markets and local CSAs began to proliferate, retail stores and restaurants began to label locally sourced products as such, and schools began developing "farm to school" relationships with local growers. Suburban communities lifted restrictions on backyard livestock production, and Williams-Sonoma launched a new "Agrarian" line of home products that included $1,300 chicken coops and $70 vintage watering cans (pre-scuffed to give an impression of frequent use).

The local food movement has brought a significant expansion in direct farmer-to-customer sales. Between 1994 and 2012, the number of local farmers' markets in the United States increased from 1,755 to 7,864, and between 2001 and 2010 the number of CSAs increased from 761 to 2,500. In 2010, Wal-Mart, the largest grocer in the United States with $120 billion a year in food sales, pledged to increase the locally sourced share of its fruit and vegetable sales up to 9 percent by 2015. Safeway and other chains moved in the same direction.

There is no single agreed-upon definition of "local" food. The U.S. Department of Agriculture describes a food product as local or regional if it either comes from in-state, or from within a 400-mile radius, a distance four times as great as the movement's leaders would prefer. When labeling its products "locally grown," Wal-Mart uses the in-state definition. Whole Foods uses a time-in-transit standard (7 or fewer hours of travel by car or truck) but allows individual stores to use tighter rules if they wish.

What explains the growing market for local food?

Surveys reveal that consumers are willing to pay more for locally grown food because they perceive it to be fresher, because they want to support their local economy, because they want to know where their food did or did not come from, and also because they want to support small farms as opposed to factory farms. Some consumers also believe local food will be more nutritious and safer to eat than supermarket food.

The nutritional advantages can be real, because locally grown food sold at a farmers' market is more likely to have been picked recently and closer to optimal ripeness. As a disadvantage, most local food is only available in season, so in colder regions an effort to buy locally can be an excellent supplement to good nutrition during warm months, but less so in winter. Regarding safety, locally grown food is ordinarily just as safe as supermarket food, but seldom any safer. Spoilage of meat is as much of a problem when buying from small local producers as when buying from supermarkets. Produce from farmers' markets is sometimes less thoroughly washed. Local raw-milk cheese may be just as likely to carry listeria. Small local producers often lack the costly equipment used by larger operations to protect against microbial contamination. In 2010, local growers who make direct sales demanded from Congress—and received—an exemption from some new food safety requirements that others would have to observe.

Apart from cost, nutrition, safety, or convenience, direct food sales from farmers to local consumers do bring important social benefits. Some consumers purchase food from farmers' markets or CSAs simply to add a satisfying social dimension to their weekly food routine. Sociologists calculate that shoppers will have on average ten times as many conversations at a farmers' market compared to a supermarket. Journalist Michael Pollan, a leading voice in the local food movement, observes that when people shop at a farmers' market they become less like consumers and more like neighbors. "In many cities and towns," he wrote in 2010, "farmers' markets have taken on (and not for the first time) the function of a lively new public square."

Political support for the local food movement has grown strong enough in the United States to inspire a number of supporting federal programs, including a Community Food Project Grants Program for CSAs, a voucher program for low-income seniors to shop at farmers' markets, a Commodity Facilities Program to support construction of farmers' markets, and a USDA initiative named "Know Your Farmer, Know Your Food," designed in 2009 to connect consumers with local producers by supporting community food projects and farm-to-school programs. Also in 2009, advocates for local food persuaded First Lady Michelle Obama to plant a vegetable garden on the White House lawn. At the state level, Vermont is now financing a mobile slaughter unit for small-scale poultry processing, and Alaska has a procurement law for state agencies requiring food purchases to be in-state so long as the cost is no more than 7 percent above the out-of-state price.

Home and community gardens, farmers' markets, CSAs, co-ops, and farm-to-school programs are unlikely ever to constitute more than a tiny share of total food sales in the United States. In 2008, according to the USDA, such sales represented only about 1.6 percent of the U.S. market for all agricultural products. The dominant long-term commercial trend remains one of globalization, not localization. Much of the food grown in the United States continues to be exported, and the imported share of food consumption has increased as well, from 12 percent in 1990 up to 17 percent by 2009. Worldwide, the total volume of agricultural products traded internationally has increased more than sixfold since 1950, in part because ocean freight shipping rates have fallen by 60 percent. Improvements in product protection and shipping technologies such as refrigerated containers and flash freezing, plus falling air freight rates, allow even highly perishable products to move internationally today. Consumers are willing to pay more for local foods, but they also want fresh fruits and vegetables available at the supermarket year-round. Food markets have been responsive enough to supply more of both.

What is urban agriculture?

City dwellers in the United States have long planted gardens wherever space is available, particularly during World War II, when "Victory Gardens" were officially promoted as a supplement to the nation's food supply. In developing countries today, recent migrants from the countryside almost always bring gardening habits—and even livestock production—into the city with them. Urban agriculture in the United States today is being promoted as part of the local food movement, with patterns of growth that take both an outdoor and an indoor form.

Outdoor urban gardening has spread rapidly in cities such as Detroit and Chicago, where out-migration and industrial decline have left a patchwork of vacant lots. These are often the same neighborhoods where supermarkets selling fresh vegetables can seem hard to find, so the residents of these communities, either spontaneously or with municipal support, increasingly turn to food gardening. In Detroit, neighborhood gardeners have filled up thousands of vacant lots in the city with small vegetable plots. Urban gardening for personal use typically requires no permit, while farming for commercial sale quite often does, and commercial animal production may be prohibited entirely, on public health grounds. In other cities where land values remain high, the spread of urban gardens and farming has been more limited. For example, while New York City mayor Michael Bloomberg has tasked city agencies to identify vacant parcels that might be reclaimed for gardening, the actual number of community gardens in New York has fallen by half since the mid-1980s. Outdoor city gardens on vacant land can provide nutritious food and healthy exercise, but there can also be safety risks from soil contamination on industrial lots, or from the use of waste water for irrigation, odors from composting, and hazards from the exposure of food to vehicle emissions.

An entirely different form of urban agriculture is indoor production in vertical greenhouses, called "vertical farming."

While not yet a proven commercial option, high-rise vegetable production systems are currently being piloted in a number of locations, including a 12-story triangular tower in Sweden (a "Plantagon") where leafy green vegetable plants will grow in boxes while traveling slowly around the sunny perimeter of the glass structure, on tracks from the top floor to the bottom floor, where the boxes are harvested, replanted, then lifted mechanically back to the top. Such systems can be located close to urban markets and can operate year-round, immune from weather risk. But these advantages may not be able to offset the high capital and energy costs.

Does local food help slow climate change?

Claims that local food production cut greenhouse gas emissions by reducing the burning of transportation fuel are usually not well founded. Transport is the source of only 11 percent of greenhouse gas emissions within the food sector, so reducing the distance that food travels after it leaves the farm is far less important than reducing wasteful energy use on the farm. Food coming from a distance can actually be better for the climate, depending on how it was grown. For example, field-grown tomatoes shipped from Mexico in the winter months will have a smaller carbon footprint than local winter tomatoes grown in a greenhouse. In the United Kingdom, lamb meat that travels 11,000 miles from New Zealand generates only one-quarter the carbon emissions per pound compared to British lamb because farmers in the United Kingdom raise their animals on feed (which must be produced using fossil fuels) rather than on clover pastureland.

When food does travel, what matters most is not the distance traveled but the travel mode (surface versus air), and most of all the load size. Bulk loads of food can travel halfway around the world by ocean freight with a smaller carbon footprint, per pound delivered, than foods traveling just a short distance but in much smaller loads. For example, 18-wheelers carry much larger loads than pickup trucks so they can move food 100 times as far while burning only one-third as much gas per pound of food delivered. Local growers who move food around in small loads by pickup are burning far more fossil fuel, per tomato delivered, than large growers from out of state who move food around in bulk.

What is the difference between local food and slow food?

The slow food movement (whose logo is a snail) originated in Italy in 1986, initially as a backlash against the introduction of fast foods into Europe. Slow food advocates work to preserve local cuisines and gastronomic traditions, including heirloom varieties of local grains and breeds of livestock. They view this as one way to fight back against both the loss of culture and the frenzy brought to us by fast foods, supermarkets, and global agribusiness. Slow food is now an important international social movement with roughly 100,000 members organized into more than 1,300 local chapters (called *convivia*) in 150 different countries. Each *convivium* promotes local farmers, local food artisans, and local Taste Workshops.

The United States has far less gastronomic tradition to preserve than Italy, but in 2008, more than 60,000 people attended a slow food national gathering in San Francisco, savoring local cuisines at taste pavilions and celebrating the planting of an urban garden in front of city hall. In 2010, thousands of local slow food supporters participated in a national "Dig In," by first gardening together and then eating together.

What explains the loyalty of some groups to organic, local, or slow food?

Groups in society have always sought solidarity through the foods they eat, or the foods they agree not to eat. Within most religious traditions, patterns of food consumption are carefully regulated. Judaism has strict rules, called *kashrut*, to specify what may and may not be eaten. In Islam, foods are divided into *haram* (forbidden) and *halal* (permitted). Hindus who embrace the concept of *ahimsa* do not eat meat to avoid doing violence to animals. In Roman Catholicism, fasting is required and meat consumption is discouraged at certain times in the religious calendar.

In today's less religious world, we should not be surprised to see the emergence of new food rules to express solidarity around secular values. The new rules that emerge (organic, local, or slow) may be attractive or practical only for relatively small subcategories of citizens, or perhaps only for a small part of the diet of those citizens, but the exclusivity and difficulty of the rule can be part of its attraction. The goal is to express through the diets we adopt a solidarity with others who share our identity, our values, or our particular life circumstances. The scientific foundation for these modern food rules may at times be weak, but the social value can nonetheless be strong.

13

FOOD SAFETY
AND GENETICALLY
ENGINEERED FOODS

How safe is America's food supply?

In rich countries, the food choices available in supermarkets and restaurants are almost always free from dangerous levels of toxic or microbial contamination. Even when they are not healthful or nutritious, they at least can be considered "safe." In the United States, food safety risks are low—in fact, lower than ever—yet as societies become more affluent, even a small risk can be seen as unacceptable, so the public demand for strong food safety policies continues to increase. Food safety lapses remain favorite stories in the popular media, and both food companies and food retailers know they will pay a heavy price if a lapse can be traced back to them.

Food can be a source of more than 200 known diseases, exposing us to viruses, bacteria, parasites, toxins, metals, and prions (as in the case of mad cow disease). Food illness symptoms can range from mild gastroenteritis to life-threatening neurologic, hepatic, and renal syndromes. According to the Centers for Disease Control and Prevention (CDC) in Atlanta, Georgia, food-borne diseases cause approximately 3,000 deaths in the United States each year. Three pathogens, salmonella, listeria, and toxoplasma, are responsible for approximately 30 percent of the deaths. Children under the age of four are sickened by food more than any other age group, but adults over the age of 50 suffer more hospitalizations and deaths.

The changing frequency of food-borne illness in any large population is difficult to monitor and measure. Mild cases often go unreported, so official frequency counts will be heavily dependent on the intensity of surveillance. Nationally since 1996, the CDC has attempted to track food-borne sickness through regular surveys of more than 650 clinical laboratories around the country that serve about 46 million people in 10 different states. At the state level, surveillance is less systematic, leading to counts that are hard to compare. Food-borne illness can even be overreported, because many pathogens transmitted by food may also be spread through water or from person to person without anything being ingested at all. Specific pathogens may never be identified, creating a further possibility that an illness was unrelated to food.

America's food supply is far safer today than it was in the past, before the era of refrigeration and sanitary packaging. Surveys by the CDC show decades of steadily increasing safety, up to the present day for some common infections. For example, infections caused by E. coli O157 declined by 44 percent between 1996 and 2010, while infections from listeria declined 38 percent, and campylobacter by 27 percent. Infections from salmonella, however, were no longer declining and had even increased by 3 percent between 1996 and 2010. The CDC attributes the overall downward trend in food-borne infections to enhanced knowledge about how to prevent contaminations, cleaner slaughter methods, increased awareness in food service establishments and private homes of the risks of undercooked ground beef, and regulatory prohibition, since 1994, of any contamination of ground beef with E. coli O157.

The vast majority of hospitalizations and fatalities from food contamination today come not from large outbreaks linked to dangerous batches of products in supermarkets but instead from a steady background level of illness caused by careless handling and improper preparation inside the home. Unwashed hands, unwashed cutting boards, poorly refrigerated foods, or meats insufficiently cooked are the most frequent cause. Wider illness outbreaks still take place, but the fatalities are usually quite limited. For example, illness from bagged spinach in 2006 led to a nationwide scare and the virtual suspension of all fresh and bagged spinach sales in America, but there were only three known deaths. In 2011, listeria on melons from Colorado caused the single worst food-borne disease outbreak since 1985, but with only 33 known deaths. Consumers fear contamination in meats, but in the United States twice as many people are likely to get sick from contaminated produce versus contaminated meat.

Even if the CDC number of 3,000 annual deaths from food-borne illness is accurate, this is far fewer than the 30,000 deaths associated with obesity every year. Eating *too much* food is now a significantly greater health risk in America than eating unsafe food. Yet any illness from foods contaminated at purchase will cause public outrage, because this is an involuntary exposure to risk in contrast to risks from smoking, or overeating. Because purchasing food at supermarkets is a common experience for us all, anxieties spread quickly to vast numbers of citizens when a danger in the market is confirmed or even rumored. The unusually wide audience for these fears explains why the popular media give food illness outbreaks from product contamination such sensational coverage. Under the spotlight of media attention, government officials and politicians are always obliged to express intense concern, whatever the actual magnitude of the problem.

How do foods become contaminated?

Food is vulnerable to contamination at nearly every stage along the production and delivery chain, all the way from farm to fork. Microbial contamination of fresh produce is possible at the farm level (a problem with California lettuce and Guatemalan raspberries in the 1990s). In meat slaughter, inadequate knife sterilization and improper evisceration or hide removal can lead to contamination. Pathogens can also be introduced by unsanitary conveyor belts or unclean processing and packaging equipment. Farther down the chain in wholesale and retail outlets, inadequate refrigeration is a problem. In restaurants, cooks who do not wash their hands introduce risks.

Private industries increasingly seek to control such contamination through the use of what are called Hazard Analysis and Critical Control Point (HACCP) systems. These systems, first innovated by the Pillsbury Company in the 1960s, identify where hazards might enter the food production process and specify the stringent actions needed at each separate step to prevent this from occurring. In 1996, the U.S. Department of Agriculture (USDA) issued its own rule for HACCP systems for meat and poultry, a requirement that is costly for industry, but effective, as suggested by the 44 percent reduction in *E. coli* 0157 contamination seen since 1996.

Food adulteration is a related issue. Consumers will spurn foods if they are found to contain ingredients not indicated on the label—especially ingredients of lower quality—even if the food is perfectly safe to consume. Ground meats are often sold containing safe ingredients that would nonetheless surprise and even anger consumers, if they knew. In 2012, many American consumers were distressed to learn, from an ABC news broadcast, that a product extracted from slaughterhouse beef trimmings known as "pink slime" was being used in ground beef. There was no demonstrated safety risk, but some companies tried to reassure consumers by halting the sale of ground beef that used this filler. In 2013 in Europe, a discovery that some ground beef products contained more than 1 percent horse meat led to the withdrawl of millions of products from supermarkets in Ireland, the United Kingdom, France, Italy, Spain, Sweden, and Romania.

Who regulates food contamination in the United States?

At the federal level, responsibility for food safety is divided between the Food and Drug Administration (FDA) inside the U.S. Department of Health and Human Services and the Food Safety and Inspection Service (FSIS) inside the Department of Agriculture. The FSIS is responsible for meat and poultry, while the FDA is responsible for everything else. State public health agencies and city and county health departments also play a continuous monitoring role. Inadequate coordination among these various agencies has been a persistent concern, and in 1998, the Clinton administration created a Food Outbreak Response Coordinating Group inside the Department of Health and Human Services, designed to increase communication and coordination. The division of labor between the FSIS and the FDA has nonetheless remained problematic. For example, frozen pizzas are inspected by the FDA if they are cheese and by the FSIS if they are pepperoni. The FSIS is responsible for chickens, but the FDA is responsible for the eggs.

Food industries in the United States are generally comfortable with strong FDA safety regulations. Following a prominent salmonella outbreak in eggs in 2010, which sickened people in all 50 states (though no one died), Congress passed a new food safety law (the Food Safety Modernization Act, the first major change since 1938), giving the FDA new responsibilities to inspect food-processing plants and farms for prevention purposes, rather than just tracing contamination after it occurs. This new law had bipartisan support from Republicans as well as Democrats and from food industries as well as from consumer protection advocates. Food industries liked the law because it offered help in preventing costly product recalls. Following the 2006 *E. coli* spinach outbreak, traced to a single farm, total retail sales of bagged spinach dropped $202 million over the following 68-week period. After a 2009 salmonella contamination in peanut butter (traced to a single processing plant in Georgia), Kellogg had to recall peanut-containing products worth $70 million. Big food companies typically resist greater regulation in health or labeling, but for self-protection they welcome assistance from the FDA in preserving food safety.

In fact, something of a de facto partnership between consumer advocates and big food companies surfaced in 2012, when budget cutters in the House of Representatives threatened to deny the FDA the funds it would need to implement the new 2010 law. This threat was turned back by a joint lobbying effort by consumer protection advocates plus a range of big food trade associations, including the Grocery Institute, the Snack Food Association, and the Produce Marketing Association. In the end, the budget for the FDA's new food safety program was increased rather than cut, and in early 2013 the agency proposed a sweeping array of new rules covering all aspects of growing and harvesting produce, including threats from animal manure, worker hygiene, and water use. The compliance cost was estimated at $460 a year for U.S. farmers and $1.2 billion a year for food processors.

Is food safety an issue in international trade?

Food safety often emerges as a concern in international trade, but the risks are sometimes exaggerated by those seeking to protect domestic producers from foreign competition. Imported foods from countries with lax safety standards, such as China, are a genuine concern. The United States imports more than $5 billion worth of food products from China every year, mostly seafood, juices, and pickled, dried, or canned vegetables. Prior to the enactment of a new food safety law in 2009, China had a notoriously bad food safety record. In 2008, infant formula and other milk products in China were found contaminated with melamine, an industrial chemical. Chinese peaches were found preserved with sodium metabisulfite, rice was contaminated with cadmium, noodles were flavored with ink and paraffin, mushrooms were treated with fluorescent bleach, and cooking oil was recycled from street gutters.

Fortunately for importers of Chinese food products, most of these poorly regulated food products have always been excluded from export channels. Chinese authorities work hard to control the safety of products that enter the world market by maintaining separate certification both for exporters and for the farms that supply them. A second line of defense for the United States is the FDA, which physically inspects only 2 percent of food imports into the United States but screens all imports electronically using an automated system that helps identify products posing the greatest risk. The FDA has offices in China—in Beijing, Shanghai, and Guangzhou—tasked with identifying potential food safety problems before shipments depart for the United States. Federal funding for surveillance of the nation's food supply increased after the 9/11 attacks, following enactment of a 2002 Bioterrorism Preparedness and Response Act, which deputized the Department of Homeland Security to assist in enforcing FDA standards, especially at ports of entry into the country.

When imported foods are found to be unsafe, the political reaction is swift and often excessive. In 1989, when the FDA announced that it had found two grapes from Chile contaminated with cyanide, it banned all imports of Chilean fruit, costing Chilean exporters more than $400 million. In 2001, the U.S. Department of Agriculture banned $278 million in annual imports of live hogs and uncooked animal products from Europe, to stem the spread of foot-and-mouth disease; the motives seemed mixed, because U.S. meat producers had been seeking such a ban for years to punish Europe for refusing to accept hormone-treated meat from the United States. In 2011 when an outbreak of E. coli in German sprouts killed 53 people, nearly all in Germany, the Germans initially tried to blame the outbreak on cucumbers from Spain. This damaged the reputation of Spanish exporters, costing them $200 million a week in lost sales. Russia then banned the import of all fresh vegetables from the entire European Union.

Does the industrialization of agriculture make food less safe?

The industrialization of agriculture does not make food more dangerous overall, but it does present new kinds of safety risks. In the past, food contamination outbreaks were more frequent but were localized and small scale; today, outbreaks are far less frequent (per unit of production) yet much harder to contain in one local area when they do occur. Outbreaks spread quickly today to multiple states, attracting national media attention and creating an impression that our modern food system is less safe than a more compartmentalized or localized alternative.

For example, the worst food safety lapse in recent United States history was a 2011 outbreak of listeria in cantaloupe, traced to a single packing shed in Colorado. It sickened 123 people in 26 states and actually killed 33. Yet the 33 fatalities from this largest industrial farming failure were just a tiny fraction of that year's 3,000 estimated fatalities from food-borne illness overall. Most fatalities from unsafe food still take place due to highly localized lapses, frequently inside private homes. Localized and traditional systems fail more often because they are less able to afford state-of-the-art technical options for food supply protection.

Is irradiated food safe?

One method for reducing or eliminating harmful bacteria, insects, and parasites in food is to irradiate the food with brief exposures to X-rays, gamma rays, or an electron beam. This technique has been known for the better part of a century, yet it remains rarely used in the United States. The Food and Drug Administration approved irradiation as safe and effective for use on poultry in 1992, and on meat in 1997, but it is rarely used because it makes the meat more costly and because the industry fears an adverse consumer response to the word "radiation." In the United States, irradiated foods must be labeled with a symbol, plus the words "treated with irradiation." In 2001, the CDC estimated that if half the nation's meat and poultry supply were irradiated, the result would be 900,000 fewer cases of food-borne illness and 350 fewer deaths. Advocates for irradiation observe that the technique has been judged safe by the government and might have killed the salmonella that reached grocery store shelves early in 2009 in peanut butter and peanut paste. Critics say that irradiation would only be used by private companies to hide the filthy condition of their plants.

What is genetically modified food?

Nearly all foods come from plants and animals with genes that have been modified over time through human interventions such as on-farm selection of seeds, or scientific plant breeding. In current usage, however, the term "genetically modified" is reserved for plants or animals modified through genetic engineering, also known as transgenic science or recombinant DNA (rDNA) science. Genetic engineering, first practiced in 1973, provides a method for modifying plants and animals not through controlled sexual reproduction but instead by moving individual genes physically from a source organism directly into the living DNA of a target organism. The value of this technique comes from its precision and its ability to use a wider pool of genetic resources. For example, genes carrying a specific trait to resist insect damage can be moved from a soil bacterium named Bt into a corn plant or into a cotton plant. The modified versions of these plants are known as Bt corn and Bt cotton. Alternatively, genes that direct a plant to produce beta-carotene (a precursor of vitamin A, which helps prevent blindness) can be moved from a daffodil plant into a rice plant, resulting in something called "Golden Rice."

The first engineered crop approved for commercial sale was a tomato with extended shelf life (the FlavrSavr tomato), marketed by the Calgene Company in 1994, following regulatory approval by the FDA. Then, in 1995, the Monsanto

Company secured approval for sale in the United States of Roundup Ready soybean plants, engineered to resist the herbicide glyphosate (sold by Monsanto under the trade name Roundup), reducing the cost to farmers of weed control. With one application of glyphosate, the weeds would die, but the soybean plants would not. By 1996, Monsanto's Bt corn and Bt cotton had also been approved for commercial use in the United States. The European Union also approved a number of genetically engineered crops both for human consumption and for planting in 1995–1996, including soybean, maize (corn), and canola; Japan approved soybean and tomato; Argentina approved soybean and maize; Australia approved cotton and canola; and, in 1995–1996, Mexico approved soybean, canola, potato, and tomato.

How are genetically engineered foods regulated?

Each national government has its own system for approving the planting and consumption of genetically engineered crops and foods. The United States, from the start, regulated genetically engineered crops and foods in much the same manner that it regulated conventional crops and foods, in keeping with a 1987 National Academy of Sciences finding that there was no evidence of "unique hazards" from the modification of plants using rDNA methods versus other methods. All new crops in the United States, including genetically engineered crops, are subject to regulation for biosafety (safety to the biological environment, especially to other agricultural crops and animals) by the Animal and Plant Health Inspection Service (APHIS) of the Department of Agriculture. If a crop has been engineered to produce a pesticide (such as Bt), the Environmental Protection Agency (EPA) must give its approval. The FDA is the agency that reviews new genetically engineered crops for food safety. The FDA considers the genetically engineered varieties of familiar foods to be no less safe than the conventional varieties of those same foods, so long as the engineering process has not introduced a new or unfamiliar toxicant, nutrient, or allergenic protein. Technology developers consult with the FDA to share the results of their own safety testing (the consultation is voluntary, but all developers do it); then they can put the new product on the market.

Governments in Europe have a different approach to regulating genetically engineered crops and foods, known there as genetically modified organisms (GMOs). The European approach, which many other governments around the world also follow, is to create separate laws and separate approval procedures for GMOs, and also to regulate this technology according to a significantly higher standard. Regulators in Europe can block the approval of a GMO without any evidence of an actual risk to human health or the environment, under what is known as the "precautionary principle." A new technology can be blocked simply on suspicion of a risk not yet tested for, or because of fears that a risk not found in the short run might nonetheless develop in the long run.

Despite this more precautionary approach, regulatory authorities in Europe, acting through the European Union, did approve a number of GMO foods and crops in 1995–1996, as mentioned above. Opinion in Europe then soured following a major food safety crisis linked to "mad cow disease" in the United Kingdom, a crisis entirely separate from GMOs but one that undercut citizen confidence in government food safety regulators. European regulators needed to restore their credibility with consumers, so they became more cautious toward all food technologies, especially GMOs. In 1998, yielding to demands from European activist groups such as Greenpeace and Friends of the Earth, they imposed an informal moratorium on any new approvals of GMOs. A number of European governments even began rejecting GMOs that had earlier been approved by EU authorities.

Finally, in 2004, the European Union introduced a new set of regulations intended to reassure consumers through strict labeling and tracing in the marketplace of any approved

GMO foods. Henceforth, all GMO products with as much as 0.9 percent transgenic content would have to carry an identifying label, and operators in the food chain handling approved GMOs would have to maintain audit trails, for at least five years, showing where each GM product came from and to whom it had been sold. Instead of reassuring consumers, these tight regulations strengthened the popular impression that the technology must be dangerous in some way. Food companies in Europe responded by voluntarily taking GMO ingredients out of their products, in order to avoid any stigmatizing label.

How widespread are genetically engineered foods?

Since 1995, the global area planted to GMO crops has expanded at a steady rate, reaching 170 million hectares by 2012. Still, the uptake remains limited both by geography and by crop variety. As of 2012, only 17 countries worldwide were planting more than 100,000 hectares of GMO crops, and 8 of those countries were in the Western Hemisphere. The top three countries were the United States (69 million hectares), Brazil (37 million hectares), and Argentina (24 million hectares). These top three Western Hemisphere countries, in other words, were planting more than three-quarters of all the GMOs being grown commercially worldwide.

The varieties of GMO crops grown commercially were also limited. Roughly 95 percent of the global area planted to GMOs is planted to just three crops: soybean (47 percent), maize (32 percent), and cotton (14 percent). Soybean and maize are grown in most countries for livestock feed, and cotton is an industrial crop. Very little land area has been devoted so far to growing GMO crops for direct human food consumption.

Even in the United States, the leading GMO producer, anxieties regarding consumer resistance have blocked the commercialization of most GMO food crops. It is estimated that roughly 70 percent of foods in the United States contain some ingredients from GMOs, but most of those ingredients are derivative products from soy or maize including oil, meal, sweeteners and starch. As of 2012, there was no GMO wheat or rice being grown commercially anywhere, and the only GMO fruits or vegetables grown commercially were papaya and summer squash. GMO potatoes were grown on 25,000 acres in the United States between 1999 and 2001, but then cultivation was voluntarily suspended when food service chains such as McDonald's and Burger King told suppliers they did not want to be accused by activists of serving GMO french fries. GMO tomatoes were also cultivated commercially in the United States between 1998 and 2002, but as consumer anxieties increased, they too were voluntarily withdrawn.

In most countries, the absence of GMO crop production reflects direct regulatory blockage. In all of Sub-Saharan Africa, as of 2012, the only two countries where it was legal for farmers to plant any GMO crops were the Republic of South Africa and Burkina Faso, and in Burkina the only crop legal to plant was cotton, an industrial crop. In much of Sub-Saharan Africa, it is not yet legal even to do research on GMO crops. Both India and China have invested public resources in developing GMO crops, but so far the only crop approved for cultivation in India and the only GMO crop widely cultivated in China is Bt cotton. Technical biosafety committees in these countries approved two new GMO food crops in 2009 (eggplant in India and rice in China), but in India the approval was immediately blocked through the intervention of the environment minister, and in China, as of 2012, no GMO rice had actually been commercialized. The Philippines does plant GMO maize, but it is used primarily for animal feed.

Why do some people resist GMOs?

Opposition to genetically engineered foods and crops is framed by some as a defense of food safety or environmental safety, by others as a defense of the rights of traditional farming communities, and by still others as resistance against the profit-making companies that develop and patent the technology. Others object because they think that the technology has not been adequately regulated, or because there is not yet any requirement (at least in the United States) that GMO foods be labeled in the marketplace.

These concerns are frequently fueled by sensational claims and charges. Critics assert that GMOs produce sterile seeds, forcing farmers to buy seeds every year. Others believe that GMOs kill butterflies, create superbugs or superweeds, and threaten biodiversity. Others believe that GMOs require increased use of chemical sprays. Others believe that rats that were fed GMOs have developed tumors. Still others believe that biotechnology companies—specifically Monsanto—will harass or sue innocent farmers for patent violations if GMO seeds blow into their fields. Others believe that the pollen from GMO crops on neighboring farms will compromise the certification of organic farmers. Others believe that GMO crops are responsible for farmer suicides in India.

Defenders of GMOs have shown that none of these specific charges are true. Regarding the environmental concerns, GMO corn pollen can certainly kill monarch butterfly caterpillars in laboratory experiments, but studies conducted by the EPA reveal that under dispersed field conditions the risk is "negligible." Regarding superweeds and superbugs, for many decades agriculture has suffered from crop pests more difficult to kill because they have evolved to resist chemical sprays, but this problem comes from the use of the chemical, not the GMO, and some GMOs, such as Bt crops, allow farmers to protect against insects while using fewer chemical sprays.

Nor are the food safety risks so far alleged for GMOs backed by scientific evidence. In Britain in 1998, the media gave loud play to the results of a laboratory experiment in which GMO potatoes were fed to rats, supposedly with damaging health effects, but the Royal Society later issued a statement saying that it was wrong to conclude anything from the experiment due to flaws in its design, and the results have never been replicated by scientists using a proper study design. A study done in Austria in 2008 purported to find lower reproduction rates among mice that had been fed with GMO corn, but when the Scientific Panel on Genetically Modified Organisms of the European Union reviewed the study, it found calculation errors, inconsistencies in treating the data, and an error in the method of calculating numbers of young mice (per pair rather than per delivering pair). The panel said that this nullified any conclusions that might be drawn from the study. Then in 2012, a French study supposedly showed that rats were more likely to develop tumors if they ate genetically modified corn sprayed with weed killer, but the European Food Safety Agency challenged the study immediately, concluding that it was "of insufficient scientific quality to be considered as valid for risk assessment." It turned out that the rats used in the experiment had been specifically bred for a propensity to develop tumors.

Do genetically engineered crops strengthen corporate control?

Many charges against GMOs are based on fears that they change our traditional relationship to food by weakening individual control and strengthening corporate control. Some aspects of this charge are easy to reject. For example, the widely held belief that GMOs have sterile seeds is simply false. GMO seeds do not contain so-called terminator genes, and they are just as easy to replicate as non-GMO seeds. Indeed, the technology has often been spread by farmers who get the seeds, take them across a border (e.g., from Argentina into Brazil), and then start planting and replanting them even without official permission.

The fear that corporations will use patents on GMO seeds to gain excessive control is also an exaggeration. This risk does not apply in most developing countries, because intellectual property laws in those countries do not permit the patenting of seeds. In countries that do permit seed patents, such as the United States and Canada, biotechnology companies like Monsanto will indeed go to court to defend their patent rights, and this creates something new for farmers to deal with. Yet nearly all commercial farmers in the United States and Canada have been more than willing to purchase GMO seeds every year rather than violate patents by saving and replanting seeds from the last year's crop. This is because the purchased seeds are of higher quality and usually deliver cost savings that more than offset the price.

GMO critics frequently cite the case of Canadian canola farmer Percy Schmeiser, who in 1999 was sued by Monsanto for planting patented Roundup Ready canola seeds without a license. It was discovered that 50–95 percent of Schmeiser's canola contained Monsanto's gene, so he was unable to convince the Canadian Supreme Court that the seeds blew in from the road, and he lost the case. Schmeiser countersued Monsanto for libel, trespass, and the contamination of his fields but lost that case too. Monsanto does use aggressive legal tactics against those whom it suspects of intentional patent infringement, but the company does not have a record of going to court over trace amounts of GMOs introduced accidentally or through cross-pollination.

The danger that accidental cross-pollination could lead to the de-certification of organic farmers is also mostly imagined. The simple presence of detectable GMO material in a crop does not constitute a violation of the national organic standard in the United States. As long as the grower has not intentionally planted GMO seed, organic certification cannot be revoked.

A more legitimate concern in the United States is that GMO foods are sold in the market without an identifying label, whereas in most other advanced industrial countries, and in many developing countries as well, labels are legally mandated. Opinion research has consistently shown that a strong majority of Americans want mandatory labels on GMOs, but the Food and Drug Administration has consistently held that there is no justification for requiring labels so long as the GMO process has introduced nothing significant for human health or safety, such as a toxin, an allergen, or a different nutrient property. A petition campaign named "Just Label It" has sought to persuade the FDA to change its position, and in 2012 a California ballot issue named Proposition 37 to mandate labels on GMO foods was launched with strong popular support. This measure failed by a vote of 53 percent to 47 percent after a number of food and biotechnology companies (led by Monsanto, Kraft Foods, PepsiCo, and Coca-Cola) waged a $46 million public campaign in opposition. Supporters of mandatory labeling vowed to try again in other states, based on a consumer's "right to know." In the past, however, federal judges have struck down measures that mandate labels in response to consumer curiosity alone, tating that voluntary labeling schemes are available under such circumstances.

Early in 2013, the Whole Foods grocery chain announced that it would require mandatory labels in its stores for all foods with GMO content by 2018. Other private food and food retail companies also met to strategize, fearing more labeling pressures and hoping to avoid a patchwork of separate regulations state by state. Momentum for mandatory labels was building, but Congress, the FDA, and the federal court system were likely to have the last word.

Are GMO foods and crops safe?

When GMO foods and crops were first placed on the market in the 1990s, some scientific bodies—for example, the British Medical Association (BMA)—initially held back from expressing an official opinion on the new technology. By the early 2000s, however, all of the most important science academies around the world—including the BMA—had concluded that there was no evidence of any new risk to human health or the environment from any of the GMO foods or crops that had been placed on the market up to that point.

This remains the official position of the Royal Society in London, the BMA, the French Academy of Sciences, and the German Academies of Science and Humanities. It is also the official position of the International Council for Science (ICSU), the Organisation for Economic Co-operation and Development (OECD) in Paris, the World Health Organization (WHO), and the Food and Agriculture Organization (FAO) of the United Nations. In 2010, the Research Directorate of the European Union produced a report that went so far as to state that, "biotechnology, and in particular GMOs, are not per se more risky than e.g. conventional plant breeding technologies."

Many skeptics are not persuaded by the absence of credible scientific evidence of new risks. They invoke the precautionary slogan, "Absence of evidence is not the same thing as evidence of absence." GMO defenders respond that if you spend more than a dozen years looking for evidence of a new risk and fail to find it, that may not be proof of absence (because nobody can prove a negative), but it does count as evidence of absence.

At a deeper psychological level, many skeptics resist GMO foods and crops not because new risks are present, but instead because, to them as consumers, new benefits are largely absent. The first generation of GMO crops to come on the market helped farmers control weeds and insects at lower cost, but these GMOs did not provide a visible direct benefit to food consumers. GMO maize and GMO soybeans did not look any better, taste any better, or nourish any better, and they did not make food noticeably cheaper in Europe or the United States. In the absence of a visible direct benefit, ordinary consumers saw nothing to lose from a highly precautionary response. Consistent with this explanation is the fact that consumers—even in Europe—have not expressed any opposition to the use of genetic engineering in medical drugs, because here they can hope to get direct benefits. So long as there is some prospect for a direct benefit, they will even tolerate the many new risks that these drugs bring, as documented in clinical trials.

Could genetically engineered crops provide benefits to small farmers in developing countries?

They already have done so in significant instances, specifically for small cotton farmers in China and India. China began planting GMO cotton in 1997, and by 2010 roughly 7 million small and resource-poor farmers were growing the crop, with average income gains estimated by Clive James, from the International Service for the Acquisition of Agri-biotech Applications (ISAAA) at $220 per hectare. India has also done well with GMO cotton. One 2009 study by German-based economists Prakash Sadashivappa and Matin Qaim showed that in India farmers who adopted GMO cotton were able to reduce pesticide sprays by an average of 40 percent and realized yield gains of 30–40 percent, generating increased profits of roughly $60 per acre, even when the higher cost of the seed is taken into account. GMO cotton first became legal to plant in India in 2002, and within 10 years, more than 85 percent of cotton planted in India was GMO.

Given these significant gains from GMO cotton, it is anomalous that so many activist groups claim that the technology failed so badly as to drive farmers in India to commit suicide. When the International Food Policy Research Institute (IFPRI) investigated these claims in 2008, it found rates of suicide among Indian farmers had not increased following the introduction of GMO cotton in 2002, and it confirmed that there would be no reason to expect such an increase, given the benefit to farmers that the technology was providing.

Beyond Bt cotton, it is more difficult to establish the benefits that GMOs might provide to small farmers in the developing world, mostly because it is not yet legal for developing world farmers to plant any GMOs. Most national governments in the developing world decided to follow the European example by setting in place demanding and highly precautionary regulations governing GMOs. Some did this in the belief that European practices were the best practices (this was particularly the case for African countries with close post-colonial ties to Europe), and others had been persuaded by activist NGOs that the technology was genuinely dangerous.

These same NGOs had earlier promoted the negotiation of an international agreement—the 2000 Cartagena Protocol—governing the import and export of living GMOs (called LMOs). This agreement was modeled after the 1989 Basel Convention on the Control of Transboundary Movements of Hazardous Wastes, indicating just how suspicious the authors of the protocol were toward agricultural biotechnology. The United Nations Environment Programme (UNEP) was given the lead in helping poor countries to implement the Cartagena Protocol, and it encouraged a European-style precautionary approach.

Critics of GMOs complained originally that the technology would be of little value to the developing world because most of the GMO traits on the market (like herbicide tolerance and insect resistance) were developed in corporate labs and incorporated into crops like soybeans or yellow maize grown by large commercial farmers in rich temperate zone countries. Because the seeds had been developed by private companies, they would be too expensive for poor farmers to afford. However, when Golden Rice was developed in 2000 by a noncorporate laboratory, partly funded by the EU itself, and then offered to the developing world free of charge for humanitarian purposes, critics attacked it anyway, simply because it was a GMO. This new rice technology was developed specifically for poor tropical countries, to help reduce vitamin A deficiencies that cause some 250,000 children to go blind each year. Thanks to continuing hostility from critics and tight regulations on field trials in poor countries, Golden Rice as of 2012 was not yet available for commercial planting anywhere in the developing world.

In 2013, a U.K. environmentalist named Mark Lynas, who had helped launch the anti-GMO movement in the 1990s, took the unusual step of apologizing for his activism. Reversing his original views, he now described GMOs as a "desperately-needed agricultural innovation" that was being "strangled by a suffocating avalanche of regulations which are not based on any rational scientific assessment of risk."

14

WHO GOVERNS THE WORLD FOOD SYSTEM?

Is there a single world food system?

There is not yet a single centrally governed world food system. Food is still produced and consumed mostly inside separate and separately governed nation-states. International food markets have grown, but international trade still supplies on average only 10 percent of what people eat. One possible advantage of such a fragmented and decentralized system is that no one political authority can disrupt the whole system. The disadvantage is that when international disruptions do occur, no single individual or institution will be fully empowered or equipped to respond.

In resistance to globalization, most food around the world continues to be grown, harvested, processed, retailed, and consumed entirely within the borders of individual countries. Ninety percent of processed foods are never traded, along with 79 percent of wheat and 93 percent of rice. This pattern persists, despite the modern era of lower transportation costs, because most countries do not want to depend on other countries for their basic food supply, so they have set in place policies intended to preserve self-sufficiency.

National governments remain the dominant actors in food and farming. They are in a position to take this leading role because of the exclusive legal jurisdiction that they enjoy, as sovereign states, over farms and food markets within their borders. The differing policies that national governments pursue can generate dramatic differences in food outcomes. For example, compare food circumstances today in Haiti and the Dominican Republic. These two states cohabit the same small Caribbean island, yet in poorly governed Haiti 45 percent of all citizens are undernourished, versus just 15 percent in the better-governed Dominican Republic. Or consider North and South Korea, states that share not just a common peninsula but also a common history, national culture, and language. Because the government of South Korea has governed its national economy and its national food system with conspicuous competence over the past half century, chronic undernutrition has virtually disappeared. Because North Korea has governed its economy and food system incompetently, a million or more citizens recently died there in a devastating famine.

How do national governments exercise control?

The policy instruments used by governments to shape food and farming systems differ between rich and poor countries. In rich countries, farm sectors receive lavish income subsidies and tax credits for producers, on top of protective restrictions at the border. It is not unusual to find a significant share of total farm income dependent on public policy (18 percent of farm income in the European Union as of 2011, and 52 percent in Japan). Off the farm, food systems in rich countries are heavily shaped by national tax and competition policies (e.g., antitrust) and increasingly by stronger regulatory systems (e.g., regulations for food safety or environmental protection).

In poor countries, state interventions in the agricultural production and marketing sector are just as powerful, but they are less likely to be pro-farmer. In developing Asia, the centralized regulation of river valley irrigation systems has long given the state an instrument to control farming. National programs governing the ownership and distribution of agricultural land (including periodic efforts at redistribution under the slogan of "land reform") are also a powerful governmental prerogative. State subsidies for fertilizers, pesticides, and electricity for irrigation pumps continue to play a system-shaping role. State-run marketing systems intended to make cheaper commodities available to the poor through fair price shops are common.

In much of Africa, state-controlled production and marketing systems were originally created under colonial rule, and today's successor systems frequently preserve that control, through state-owned seed or chemical companies and "parastatal" marketing institutions that are granted near-monopoly rights by the government. The agricultural sectors in these African countries are more open to import competition and foreign direct investment than in the past, but private investment has lagged due to government restrictions, weak government investments in infrastructure, plus the failure of many governments to maintain rule of law and protect private property.

Which are the most important international organizations in the food and farming sector?

Above the level of the nation-state, the institutions of the United Nations system often take actions intended to look like "global governance," but usually these actions have little impact on core activities within the food and farming sector. For example, when food prices on the international market spiked in 2008, the secretary-general of the United Nations set up a high-level task force on the global food security crisis to produce an "action plan" prescribing an appropriate response. This gave the impression that the United Nations was taking charge, but in fact no new funding or authority was granted to the UN for this purpose, so the high-level task force had no measurable impact on either food production or consumption, and it posed no threat to national governmental control. Something similar had happened during the earlier world food crisis of 1974, when the UN created a comparably toothless committee on world food security.

A more significant international reaction to the 2008 price spike came not from the UN system but instead from the separate national governments of the major economic powers, assembled for summit meetings as the Group of 8 (G8) and the Group of 20 (G20). The G20 was established in 1999 in the wake of the East Asian financial crisis as a means to broaden international consultations beyond the smaller G8 cluster of advanced industrial states. The G20 includes emerging and transitional economic powers such as Brazil, China, India, Indonesia, South Africa, and Turkey. Both the G8 and the G20 meet on a regular basis at the head of state (or "summit") level, and these become settings in which significant national policy changes or resource commitments can be pursued. After the price spike of 2008, it was at a G8 summit meeting, in July 2009, that the world's leading powers concluded a financially significant L'Aquila pledge to increase agricultural development assistance.

Still, the purpose of the G8 and G20 is to facilitate cooperation among nation-states, not to replace or override those states. For example, when President Nicolas Sarkozy of France attempted in 2011 to use his temporary chairmanship of a G20 Summit to promote reforms in commodity futures trading, biofuels, and export policies, he was effectively blocked by the other major economic powers, including the United States, the United Kingdom, Brazil, and Russia.

Some well-established international organizations do influence global food and farming, but no more than the major national powers will allow. One example is the World Trade Organization (WTO), originally created as the General Agreement on Tariffs and Trade (GATT) at an international conference in Bretton Woods, New Hampshire, in 1944. The

WTO is headquartered in Geneva, where it provides a setting for national governments to negotiate agreements on trade, including agricultural trade. The WTO even has a Dispute Settlement Body (DSB) to adjudicate claims from member governments regarding the non-compliance of others with these international agreements. In the past decade, both the cotton policies of the United States and the sugar and GMO policies of the EU have triggered successful complaints of this kind. Deliberations within the DSB can draw on the findings of one other international institution, the Codex Alimentarius ("food code") Commission in Rome, a body created by the United Nations in 1963 to develop common global standards for safe food products and fair food trade practices. Because Codex operates by consensus, common global standards have not been achieved in controversial areas such as GMOs.

The International Monetary Fund (IMF) and the World Bank are two other international institutions created at Bretton Woods in 1944. They are largely funded by wealthy country governments and are empowered to make sizable loans to governments in developing countries, particularly those facing financial crises or struggling to create a policy environment to support sustained economic growth. The lending conditions imposed by the IMF have typically included market deregulation and an end to inflationary fiscal and monetary policies. The World Bank in the 1960s and 1970s became a significant source of lending for investments in agricultural development, but over the following three decades, it cut lending to agriculture and moved on to other concerns. Following the high world food prices of 2008, the World Bank president, Robert Zoellick, vowed to revive work in the area of agricultural development, and new loans were made, particularly to Africa. The World Bank also became home to the new Global Agriculture and Food Security Program (GAFSP), created in 2009 at the insistence of the G20, but national governments fell short in the resources contributed to this fund. The IMF and the World Bank are both headquartered in Washington, D.C., and have traditionally embraced a so-called Washington Consensus that emphasizes the role of free markets and private investments, as opposed to state planning, market controls, and government subsidies.

Specific to food and agriculture, there are three "Rome institutions" within the UN system in addition to Codex Alimentarius: IFAD, WFP, and FAO. The youngest of these is the International Fund for Agricultural Development (IFAD), established in 1977 to finance development projects focused specifically on food production and rural poverty alleviation. The IFAD is less constrained by the Washington Consensus than either the IMF or the World Bank, but at the same time it has fewer lending resources. A second Rome organization, the UN World Food Programme (WFP), was established in 1961 to manage the delivery of humanitarian food assistance to poor countries and refugee populations. Individual donor governments are still the source of nearly all international food aid, but more than half is now channeled to its destination by the WFP.

The oldest and most prominent Rome-based UN institution is the Food and Agriculture Organization (FAO). Founded in 1945, the FAO devotes most of its energy to gathering and distributing information about food and farming around the world. It also provides a forum for nations to meet to set goals, share expertise, and negotiate agreements on agricultural policy. At the FAO, agricultural ministries from member governments are often in the lead, so the organization usually places greater emphasis on food production and the prosperity of farmers than on the nutrition of consumers. Within the United Nations system, nutrition has traditionally been handled by the World Health Organization (WHO).

In the area of agricultural technology development and research, the most important international institution is the Consultative Group on International Agricultural Research (CGIAR), a network of research centers created in 1971 and chaired by the World Bank. The CGIAR eventually expanded into a network of 15 separate international centers, primarily located in the developing world and funded by government donors and private foundations, plus the World Bank. These centers attempt to extend the legacy of the original green revolution of the 1960s and 1970s by using science to develop improved seeds and more productive and sustainable farming methods in order to help farmers in the developing world.

What has limited the influence of international organizations?

The political influence of these international food and agricultural institutions differs case by case. In the 1980s and 1990s, the WTO achieved a measurable success by hosting a "Uruguay Round" of negotiations that produced some reductions in the farm subsidy policies that had been distorting trade. The Agreement on Agriculture that emerged from these negotiations in 1993 required industrial countries to convert non-tariff agricultural border protections to tariffs. The agreement imposed no restriction at all on direct cash payments to farmers, so long as those payments were de-coupled from production incentives. The agreement also prohibited direct export subsidies, but it did nothing to prevent governments from disrupting markets through export bans, which proved to be a larger concern at the time of the 2008 price spike.

Following this partly successful Uruguay Round effort, the WTO launched a new Doha Round in 2001, but these negotiations were suspended without any result seven years later, in part because of disagreements between the United States and India over exceptions to disciplines on import restrictions. The negotiations have so far not been revived, in part because higher international commodity prices have reduced the distorting effects of farm subsidy policies and have diminished the urgency of making further subsidy cuts.

Even when governments voluntarily accept policy restraints under the WTO, they sometimes fail to comply. For example, in 2005, the United States was told by the Dispute Settlement Body that elements of its cotton subsidy program were illegal under the 1993 Agreement on Agriculture, but the United States refused at first either to change its policies adequately or to pay compensation. In 2008, the U.S. Congress even passed a new farm bill explicitly preserving some of the WTO-illegal policies. Brazil eventually threatened retaliation in 2010, and the United States responded not by changing its cotton policy but instead by offering compensation payments to cotton growers in Brazil. The final outcome was ironic: United States taxpayers were now paying for cotton subsidies in two countries rather than just one.

The IMF and the World Bank had considerable influence over food and farming in the 1980s and 1990s, when they used stabilization agreements, investment loans, and "structural adjustment" loans to shape the price and market environment for farmers in poor developing countries. Yet the policy changes they hoped to induce were sometimes small or just temporary. In 1994, the World Bank completed a study of 29 governments in Sub-Saharan Africa that had undergone structural adjustment and found that 17 of those 29 had reduced the overall tax burden they placed on farming, but some, because of persistently overvalued exchange rates, had actually increased that burden. Only 4 of the 29 had eliminated parastatal marketing boards for major export crops, and none of the 29 had set in place both agricultural and macroeconomic policies that measured up to World Bank standards. Later, the International Food Policy Research Institute (IFPRI) found that many of the reforms undertaken in response to World Bank pressures were reversed when conditions changed, or in response to external shocks.

The World Bank diminished its own influence over agriculture beginning in the 1980s, when it began to cut the total value of its lending in that sector. Between 1978 and 2006, the agricultural share of World Bank lending fell from 30 percent to only 8 percent. In 2005, the World Bank president, Paul Wolfowitz, even admitted in an offhand comment, "My institution's largely gotten out of the business of agriculture." To explain this withdrawal of lending for agriculture, officials at the World Bank claimed that it was the borrowing country governments who had changed their priorities, but priorities at the Bank had changed as well. Structural adjustment lending for policy change was crowding out lending for actual investments in development.

Of the three Rome-based UN food organizations, the WFP and IFAD are frequently praised for their work, while the FAO is routinely criticized. The WFP has a proven record of preventing famine, as in the case of the 1991–1992 and 2001–2002 droughts in southern Africa. Although the WFP failed to prevent a famine in southern Somalia in 2011, the reason was blocked access due to the intransigence of an armed jihadist militia group, al Shabaab.

The reputation of the FAO for taking effective action is not as strong. In fact, it was international frustration with the FAO during the world food crisis of the 1970s that led to the creation of the IFAD in 1977. The data collection activities of the FAO are highly regarded, and in some niche areas (e.g., the integrated management of crop pests, or IPM), FAO technical advice has been world class, but its operations are heavily dominated by an oversized central bureaucracy. It has received lethargic direction over the years from a string of unresponsive leaders who have held their positions more because of their political friends than their professional competence, a pattern often encountered in UN special agencies. Looking at the budget of the FAO, more than half is spent on headquarters operations within the city of Rome, not in the developing world.

In the area of internationally funded agricultural research, the multiple centers of the CGIAR have had a four-decade history of success in developing useful new farm technologies for the developing world. The improved rice varieties originally developed by the International Rice Research Institute (IRRI) have now been released in more than 77 countries, allowing the world to more than double total rice production since 1965. Two-thirds of the developing world's total area planted to wheat is now planted to varieties that contain improvements developed by the CGIAR's International Maize and Wheat Improvement Center (CIMMYT). Nevertheless, the CGIAR has struggled since the 1990s to maintain adequate donor funding, due partly to complacency among those who thought the world's food production problems had already been solved, plus hostility from others who rejected a science-driven green revolution approach. The CGIAR's methods have not always been ideal; too much crop science at the centers is restricted to artificial conditions without being tested in actual farmers' fields, and too often the new technologies developed never reach the intended beneficiaries. The delivery of useful new production technologies to poor farmers almost always requires partnership with strong research and extension institutions at the national level, and too often in recent years these have been underfunded.

Do multinational corporations control the world food system?

Many activists assert that corporations do exercise control, through the monopoly positions they are said to enjoy in key markets and through the corrupting influence they can exercise over national governments. Intergovernmental organizations like the WTO, the IMF, and the World Bank are described by these critics as little more than the global agents of corporate control.

Assertions of corporate monopoly in the food sector usually begin with claims that 90 percent of international grain trade goes through the hands of just four private companies: Archer Daniels Midland, Bunge, Cargill, and Louis Dreyfus—known collectively as the ABCD traders. A 2012 study commissioned by the NGO Oxfam described the control of these companies as far-reaching:

> Through their roles in biofuels investment, large-scale land acquisition, and the financialization of agricultural

commodity markets, the ABCDs are at the forefront of the transformation that is determining where money in agriculture is invested, where agricultural production is located, where the produce is shipped, and how the world's population shares (or fails to share) the bounty of each harvest.

When considering such assessments, it is important to remember that only about 10 percent of world food production ever enters international trade, suggesting limits on the control available to any company that specializes in international trade. Also, despite market concentration, these four trading companies still regularly compete with each other. Finally, those who assert corporate control over grain markets seldom make a consistent argument regarding the impact of that control. Some say that the companies conspire to make international grain prices artificially low ("dumping" surplus production into poor countries), while others blame the companies for driving grain prices artificially high. In reality, grain-trading companies make money whether international prices are high or low, but they do so by skillfully responding to price changes rather than by controlling those changes.

Corporate control is also said to derive from seed patents, such as those registered by companies like Monsanto. One important limitation to this argument is that in most countries, especially developing countries, national laws do not allow patent claims on seeds. In addition, many developing world farmers buy no seeds at all, let alone patented seeds. In the Indian Punjab, 74 percent of farmers still plant their own saved seeds, and when Indian farmers do buy seeds, they have 500 private Indian seed companies to turn to, not just multinationals like Pioneer or Monsanto. Meanwhile, national biosafety regulations plus consumer resistance have tightly restricted the spread of patented seeds, even in rich countries that allow patents. For example, there are no patented GMO wheat or rice seeds on the market anywhere, not even in the United States.

In addition, corporate control over markets is weakened by competition. For example, when Monsanto tried to market a new corn seed variety called "Smartstax" in 2010, it overpriced the product and lost market shares to a competitor seed company, DuPont Pioneer. In the end, Monsanto had to reduce its price premium by 67 percent in order to win back customers, and even then it failed to recover market share.

The allegation that private food and agribusiness companies exercise influence over national governments by paying bribes does have some foundation. In one sensational exposé in 2012, investigators learned that a subsidiary of Wal-Mart in Mexico had bribed local and national officials as a pathway to building 19 large new stores, sometimes without construction permits. In some cases, Wal-Mart paid nearly a million dollars in bribes per store. In an earlier case, Monsanto was required to pay a $1.5 million fine (to the U.S. Justice Department) for having bribed an Indonesian official in 2002, to get around an environmental impact study on its cotton seeds. In this case, however, the bribe was unsuccessful because the requirement for the study was never waived, and Monsanto's cotton seeds are still not legal to plant in Indonesia. Even in countries where bribery is common, then, the bribe may not always be corporate control.

How much power do non-governmental organizations have?

International non-governmental organizations (NGOs) are influential players within food and farming sectors, especially in the developing world. Some development NGOs work almost exclusively through projects on the ground. For example, Heifer International operates roughly 900 projects in 53 different countries to promote food self-reliance through gifts of livestock and training. Other NGOs work almost exclusively through social mobilization and advocacy. One example is La Via Campesina, an organization founded at a meeting in Belgium in 1993, which advocates action on behalf of small farmers against globalized agribusiness. Via Campesina comprises about 150 local and national organizations in 70 countries, and it champions an agrarian vision of local control that it calls "food sovereignty." Greenpeace, an environmental advocacy organization based in Amsterdam, also campaigns against globalization and agribusiness, particularly against genetically engineered crops. Greenpeace claims 2.8 million members worldwide. Consumers International, a global federation of more than 240 advocacy organizations in 120 different countries, promotes consumer food safety.

In the areas of food safety and farm technology, advocacy NGOs sometimes succeed in exposing and even blocking behaviors that they dislike. In the 1970s, a network of NGOs accused Nestlé of promoting infant formula products through unethical methods, such as giving away free samples in maternity wards. An NGO-led boycott of Nestlé products, animated by the sensational charge that "Nestlé Kills Babies," eventually led to a new International Code of Marketing of Breast-milk Substitutes, which Nestlé pledged to follow in 1984. Also in the 1980s, an international NGO advocacy campaign led by the Pesticides Action Network (PAN) managed to produce an International Code of Conduct on the Distribution and Use of Pesticide, and later a binding international agreement, the Rotterdam Convention. In the 1990s, European-based NGOs spread alarms about genetically engineered crops that led in a few years to a virtual ban on the planting of those crops in Europe and to regulatory blockage in much of the rest of the world as well. In 2013, an activist from the United Kingdom who had participated in the anti-GMO campaigns, but who later changed his mind about the technology and apologized, admitted, "This was the most successful campaign I have ever been involved in."

Not all advocacy NGOs work to block things. In the area of food security, some groups like Bread for the World use information and advocacy campaigns to promote food aid and agricultural development. Others, like Oxfam, combine research and policy advocacy with actual development projects on the ground (Oxfam calls itself a "do tank"). Still others, like Catholic Relief Services, work almost exclusively delivering humanitarian relief. In the area of agricultural development, however, there are limits to what NGOs from the outside can accomplish on their own. They deliver excellent training and services but are less able to provide the expensive investments in road construction, electricity, irrigation, and agricultural research needed in many of the poorest countries. National governments supported by donor agencies with taxpayer-derived resources must take the lead here.

International NGOs in food and agriculture often export the concerns of rich countries into the developing world. In areas such as health and human rights, this can be entirely appropriate, but with agricultural technology, the concerns of the rich are not always well matched to the needs of the poor. Agricultural chemical use is clearly excessive in Europe and North America, but most agricultural scientists argue that in Africa fertilizer use needs to be increased. If European or American NGOs carry their campaigns against chemical fertilizer into Africa, where too little is currently in use, they may push local policy in the wrong direction.

What is the role of private foundations?

Independently endowed philanthropic foundations such as the Rockefeller Foundation and the Ford Foundation played an essential role in launching Asia's original green revolution in the 1960s and 1970s. Today it is the Bill and Melinda Gates Foundation that does the most to promote the green revolution cause.

The Ford Foundation, with roughly $10 billion in assets, is an important New York–based institution that provided early support to the green revolution in Asia but later moved away from promoting science-dependent approaches to farming. Although the Rockefeller Foundation had assets only one-third the size of Ford, it was more important in launching the green revolution, and it continued to stress the importance of agricultural science in developing countries long after Ford drifted away from the cause. Then, in 2006, the Bill and Melinda Gates Foundation, which had $37 billion in assets, moved decisively into grant-making in agricultural development (adopting Rockefeller as a junior partner), beginning with a $150 million joint venture called the Alliance for a Green Revolution in Africa (AGRA), chaired by former UN secretary-general Kofi Annan. This initiative centered on an effort to improve the varieties of seed available to small farmers for staple food crops in Africa. By 2012, the Gates Foundation had made grants for agricultural development totaling more than $2 billion.

By supporting seed markets, new agricultural science, and a "green revolution," the Gates Foundation knew that it would be inviting criticism from those in the NGO community who mistrusted this approach. Soon after the foundation announced its new effort, an NGO based in the United States named Food First warned that Bill and Melinda Gates were "naïve about the causes of hunger" and that their efforts would only provide "higher profits for the seed and fertilizer industries, negligible impacts on total food production and worsening exclusion and marginalization in the countryside." Many in the philanthropic community who are timid about facing hostile NGO criticism continue to shrink away from supporting science-based or market-oriented agricultural development work.

15

THE FUTURE OF FOOD POLITICS

In the future, will obesity continue to replace hunger as the world's most serious food problem?

In terms of the numbers affected, yes. In 2008, according to the World Health Organization, 500 million adults globally over the age of 20 were technically obese. If we add obese children, the total number approaches the 2008 United Nations Food and Agriculture Organization (FAO) estimate of the under-nourished population, which was 876 million. The global trend toward increased obesity has continued since 2008. Over the most recent two-decade period, the global obesity rate increased by 82 percent, according to a 2012 report from the British medical journal *The Lancet*. Projecting from current trends, scholars at Tulane University estimate that there will be 1.12 billion obese adults worldwide by 2030.

As the total number of obese people continues to increase in the years ahead, the number who are undernourished will almost certainly continue to decline. Already between 1990–1992 and 2010–2012, according to the FAO, the total number of hungry people on earth declined by 132 million in absolute terms, despite continued global population growth. The per-centage of people undernourished worldwide declined from 18.6 percent to 12.5 percent.

Consistent with this decline in hunger, most new cases of obesity in the years ahead will actually be found in the developing world. The prevalence of obesity is already high in today's rich countries, and population growth in rich countries is low or even negative, so there is less room for a future obesity increase. In today's developing and transitional countries, in contrast, populations are larger overall, they are growing much faster, and the prevalence of obesity in these countries is just now beginning its rise. We think of the United States as the nation with the largest obesity problem, but in absolute numbers China has already surpassed the United States, with 100 million obese citizens today compared to 90 million in the United States.

Finding an appropriate policy frame for responding to these realities will continue to prove difficult, in part because the obesity threat is still new. Coercive policy measures against obesity will always be problematic because in some cases there are genetic causes and because heavy weight does not always correlate with poor health. Moreover, there are many good reasons for government policies to remain focused on those with too little food rather than too much, since the former usually have fewer options for self-help. Redefining the world's food problem as obesity rather than hunger thus carries significant ethical risks. In large parts of rural Africa and South Asia, largely due to inadequate public sector investment, hunger remains the dominating food-related concern. In Sub-Saharan Africa today, there are still three times as many underweight preschool children as there are overweight preschoolers, and the absolute number of malnourished people in this region continues to rise, as the population grows while poverty reduction in the countryside continues to lag.

In the future, will food and farming systems become more localized or more globalized?

Food and farming are in many ways similar to other modern production and marketing systems. They are driven toward greater globalization by falling transportation costs, increasing income and consumption demand in previously poor countries, and lower policy barriers toward international investment and trade. Economic competition induces all production systems to cut costs through greater specialization and market exchange. Over time, individual production units shrink in number but grow in size, and products travel greater distances. Market volatility drives production units toward risk reduction through more formally structured or contracted relationships. Yet thanks to competition and continuing innovation, the prices offered to consumers usually decline. In the food sector between 1961 and 2010, the average real international price for cereals, meats, dairy, and sugar products actually declined by 40 percent.

In the future, it is unlikely that today's rich countries will move back toward food systems based less on globalization and more on localization, or based less on specialization and more on diversification. Niche markets for locally grown foods will continue to prosper and expand with purchasing power, and as consumer preferences diversify, but a preponderance of consumers will continue to use the conventional market channels that offer lower cost, greater convenience, and far greater year-round variety.

Both poor and transitional countries will become less poor, more urban, and therefore more like today's rich countries in the way that they produce and consume food. Eating habits worldwide will continue to converge toward common sets of practices, including an increased reliance on foods purchased at supermarkets; increased consumption of packaged and processed foods, frozen foods, meat, eggs, and dairy products; and also year-round consumption of more nutritious fresh fruits and vegetables. One common feature in this convergence will be a wider range of affordable eating choices, both healthy and unhealthy. Different communities and different individuals will make their food choices in different ways, leading to divergent health and nutrition outcomes, but the choices available will continue to expand for nearly all. Individual diets will continue to move away from being one's geographic or economic destiny, toward being instead a result of conscious choice.

In the future, will the spread of affluent eating habits destroy the natural environment?

The answer is yes, unless food production systems evolve rapidly toward less dependence on land, water, and chemical inputs and toward reduced dependence on natural systems such as wild fisheries. Politically fractious debates will nonetheless continue over how—and how far—modern food production systems should evolve in this direction. Productivity skeptics will call instead for more austere eating habits, including moves away from the heavy consumption of meat and animal products, and an abandonment of food production systems based on highly specialized industrial-scale operations. But commercial farming will continue to evolve in that direction.

Optimists (who would call themselves realists) will doubt the inclination of most people to move toward a vegetarian diet voluntarily, and they will not want governments to have license to coerce such an outcome. They will put more faith in the ability of agricultural science to provide ways to grow more food, and also more feed for animals, even while using less land, less water, and fewer chemicals. They point to data from the U.S. Department of Agriculture (USDA) showing that in the United States, since 1982, total farm output has increased roughly 40 percent, while annual fertilizer, herbicide, and insecticide use has actually declined. They observe that since 1980 in the United States, total corn production has doubled, while land use per bushel has declined by 30 percent and energy use per bushel has declined by 43 percent. Regulation has played only a small role in these gains; the secret has been technical improvements driven by market competition, for example, no-till farming, the use of GPS systems, and new crops that self-protect against insects.

What worries the optimists is a lag in the research investments needed to ensure that the pace of innovation will continue, especially within the less productive tropical farming systems of South Asia and Africa. All agricultural systems face highly localized challenges that can only be met through investments in local innovation. Inadequate external support for agricultural research in the poor countries of Africa, plus accelerating climate change, presents a daunting challenge. The environmental price of failing to improve Africa's low-yield farming systems will be more cutting of trees, more soil nutrients mined, more fragile lands plowed and ruined, and more wildlife habitat destroyed to accommodate a relentless spread of low-yield farming, as population continues to increase.

The global spread of more lavish eating habits will directly threaten the world's wild ocean fisheries. Increasingly affluent consumers in Asia will demand more fish. China, the world's largest seafood consumer, continues to expand its long-range fishing fleet at a time when 87 percent of global fisheries are already considered fully exploited, overexploited, or depleted. This growing threat to wild fish populations can be reduced through the production of more "farmed" fish, both in and away from saltwater, but making aquaculture environmentally sustainable and politically acceptable is still an unsolved problem. Larger investments in research and innovation may provide answers, but the skeptics will balk, wishing instead that we would only consume less.

In the future, will the politics of food remain contentious?

Yes, and it may become even more contentious. Political debates over farm policy have already moved beyond material questions, such as who owns the land or who gets the biggest subsidies, to questions of contested values, such as what a rural landscape should look like. Should farms be large-scale and specialized, or small-scale and diversified? Organic and local, or high-tech and global? Such questions will become more contentious as the number of people who actually make their living from farming continues to decline. Increasingly, it will be non-farmers without a livelihood stake in crop or livestock production who set the terms of the debate. They will bring to the table a wider range of values and motives, often divergent from those that have traditionally dominated the sector. The hard-fought distributional politics of protecting or expanding producer subsidies will continue, but it will increasingly be supplemented by a new "hard-felt" politics over what kind of farming is humane, sustainable, and just.

At the consumption end, a similar transition will take place. As food becomes increasingly safe to eat, increasingly affordable, and abundant in endless variety year-round, the concerns of consumers will also move away from issues of cost or safety toward less material concerns, including those driven by ethics and culture.

In this realm of ethics and culture, advocates for the status quo will always be on the defensive. It will never be enough for them to show that the present is better than the past. Ordinary producers and consumers in the marketplace might be comfortable with the trends they see in today's food and farm systems, but cultural critics and opinion leaders will continue to imagine and promote more attractive, or seemingly more attractive, alternatives. The result could be a growing divergence between actual commercial outcomes and the stated preferences of cultural elites. As food systems become more globalized, leaders in the cultural marketplace will continue calling for a return to local food. As modern farms continue to specialize and grow in size, cultural leaders will continue to champion a return to smaller and more diversified farms.

Will it be possible, in the future, for one set of trends in the commercial arena to coexist with an opposing set of preferences in the cultural arena? It usually falls to political leaders to resolve such tensions, typically through efforts to please both sides. In democratic systems such as the United States, the outcome in the governmental arena—so far—has been to allow food and farming systems to continue their evolution toward a larger scale, more specialization, and more internationalization, so as to continue serving consumer demands for cost savings, variety, and convenience. Industry lobbies that favor these trends have continued to hold the upper hand, and most ordinary voters seem comfortable with these trends as well. A majority of elected leaders have therefore decided, for now, not to use their tax and regulatory powers to force farming back toward a smaller, more local, more diverse, or less science-based model. They have also concluded, for now, that voters and campaign contributors will punish any attempt to reduce the range of eating choices currently enjoyed by citizens, no matter how unhealthy some of those choices might be. This is what food politics has given us for the moment, but as the twenty-first century continues to unfold, the political equilibrium of the moment will, of course, be subject to change.

SUGGESTIONS FOR FURTHER READING

Food Production and Population Growth

Bremer, Jason. *Population and Food Security: Africa's Challenge.* Population Reference Bureau, Policy Brief, 2012.

Conway, Gordon. *One Billion Hungry: Can We Feed the World?* Ithaca, NY: Cornell University Press, 2012.

Diamond, Jared. *Collapse: How Societies Choose to Fail or Succeed.* New York: Penguin, 2005.

Falcon, Walter P., and Rosamond L. Naylor. "Rethinking Food Security for the 21st Century." *American Journal of Agricultural Economics* 87, no. 5 (2005): 1113–1127.

Lappé, Frances Moore, and Joseph Collins. *Diet for a Small Planet.* New York: Ballantine Books, 1971.

Malthus, Thomas Robert. *An Essay on the Principle of Population.* Cambridge: Cambridge University Press, 1992.

Paddock, William, and Paul Paddock. *Famine, 1975! America's Decision: Who Will Survive?* Boston: Little, Brown, 1967.

United Nations. *World Population Prospects 2002: Analytical Report.* New York: United Nations, 2004.

World Bank. *World Development Report 2008: Agriculture for Development.* Washington, DC: World Bank, 2007.

The Politics of High Food Prices

Fan, Shenggen. *Halving Hunger: Meeting the First Millennium Development Goal through "Business as Usual."* Washington, DC: International Food Policy Research Institute, 2010.

Food and Agriculture Organization of the United Nations. *FAO: Hunger Portal.* http://www.fao.org/hunger/en/.

Mitchell, Donald O., Merlinda D. Ingco, and Ronald C. Duncan. *World Food Outlook.* New York: Cambridge University Press, 2008.

Pardey, P. G., J. M. Alston, and R. R. Piggott, eds. *Agricultural R&D in the Developing World: Too Little, Too Late?* Washington, DC: International Food Policy Research Institute, 2006.

United States Department of Agriculture, Economic Research Service. *Food Security Assessment, 2010–20.* Outlook Report No. GFA-21, Agriculture and Trade Reports. Washington, DC: United States Department of Agriculture, 2010.

Von Braun, Joachim. *Responding to the World Food Crisis: Getting on the Right Track.* Washington, DC: International Food Policy Research Institute, 2008.

The Politics of Chronic Hunger

Akhter, U. Ahmed, Ruth Vargas Hill, Lisa C. Smith, Doris M. Wiesmann, and Tim Frankenberger. *The World's Most Deprived: Characteristics and Causes of Extreme Poverty and Hunger.* 2020 Discussion Paper 43. Washington, DC: International Food Policy Research Institute, 2007.

Kotz, Nick. *Hunger in America: The Federal Response.* New York: Field Foundation, 1979.

Lipton, Michael. *Why Poor People Stay Poor: Urban Bias in World Development.* Cambridge, MA: Harvard University Press, 1977.

Oxfam International. *Causing Hunger: An Overview of the Food Crisis in Africa.* Briefing Paper 91. Oxford, UK: Oxfam, 2006.

Sachs, Jeffrey D., John McArthur, Guido Schmidt-Traub, Margaret Kruk, Chandrika Bahadur, Michael Faye, and Gordon McCord. "Ending Africa's Poverty Trap." *Brookings Papers on Economic Activity* 1 (2004): 117–240.

Smith, Lisa C., and Lawrence Haddad. *Overcoming Child Malnutrition in Developing Countries, Discussion Paper 30 (February)*. Washington, DC: International Food Policy Research Institute, 2000.

Thurow, Roger. *The Last Hunger Season: A Year in an African Farm Community on the Brink of Change*. New York: Public Affairs, 2012.

United States Department of Agriculture. *Household Food Security in the United States 2011*. Economic Research Report ERR-141. 2012.

The Politics of Famine

Becker, Jasper. *Hungry Ghosts: Mao's Secret Famine*. New York: Holt, 1998.

Conquest, Robert. *Harvest of Sorrow: Soviet Collectivization and the Terror Famine*. New York: Oxford University Press, 1987.

Grada, Cormac O. *Famine: A Short History*. Princeton, NJ: Princeton University Press, 2009.

Haggard, Stephan, and Marcus Noland. *Famine in North Korea: Markets, Aid, and Reform*. New York: Columbia University Press, 2009.

Natsios, Andrew. *The Great North Korean Famine*. Washington, DC: United States Institute of Peace Press, 2002.

Sen, Amartya. *Poverty and Famines: An Essay on Entitlement and Deprivation*. New York: Oxford University Press, 1983.

The Green Revolution Controversy

Altieri, Miguel. *Agroecology: The Science of Sustainable Agriculture*. 2nd ed. Boulder, CO: Westview Press, 1995.

Evenson, R. E., and D. Gollin. "Assessing the Impact of the Green Revolution, 1960 to 2000." *Science* 300 (May 2003): 758–762.

Hayami, Yujiro, and Vernon W. Ruttan. *Agricultural Development: An International Perspective*. Baltimore, MD: Johns Hopkins University Press, 1985.

Hazell, Peter, and Lawrence Haddad. *Agricultural Research and Poverty Reduction*. Food, Agriculture, and Environment Discussion Paper 34. Washington, DC: International Food Policy Research Institute, 2001.

Hazell, Peter, C. Ramasamy, and P. K. Aiyasamy. *The Green Revolution Reconsidered*. Baltimore, MD: Johns Hopkins University Press, 1991.

International Assessment of Agricultural Science, Technology, and Development. *Executive Summary of Synthesis Report*, 2008. http://www.agassessment.org/docs/IAASTD_exec_summary_JAN_2008.pdf.

Juma, Calestous. *The New Harvest: Agricultural Innovation in Africa.* New York: Oxford University Press, 2011.

Pingali, Prabhu L. "Green Revolution: Impacts, Limits, and the Path Ahead." *PNAS* 109, no. 31 (2012): 12302–12308.

Ruttan, Vernon W. "Controversy about Agricultural Technology: Lessons from the Green Revolution." *International Journal of Biotechnology* 6, no. 1 (2004): 43–54.

Williams, Robert G. *Export Agriculture and the Crisis in Central America.* Chapel Hill: University of North Carolina Press, 1986.

Food Aid, Food Power, and Development Assistance

Barrett, Christopher B., Andrea Binder, and Julia Steets, eds. *Uniting on Food Assistance: The Case for Transatlantic Cooperation.* New York: Routledge, 2012.

Barrett, Christopher B., and Daniel G. Maxwell. *Food Aid after Fifty Years: Recasting Its Role.* New York: Routledge, 2005.

Bertini, Catherine, and Dan Glickman. *2012 Progress Report on U.S. Leadership in Global Agricultural Development.* Chicago Council on Global Affairs, 2012.

Hanrahan, Charles E. *International Food Aid Provisions of the 2008 Farm Bill.* Congressional Research Service Report for Congress, July 10, 2008.

Paarlberg, Robert. *Food Trade and Foreign Policy: India, the Soviet Union, and the United States.* Ithaca, NY: Cornell University Press, 1985.

The Politics of Obesity

Institute of Medicine. *Accelerating Progress in Obesity: Solving the Weight of the Nation.* Washington, DC, 2012.

Kessler, David A. *The End of Overeating.* Emmaus, PA: Rodale Press, 2009.

Ludwig, David S. "Childhood Obesity—The Shape of Things to Come." *New England Journal of Medicine* 357, no. 23 (2007): 2325–2327.

Oliver, J. Eric. *Fat Politics: The Real Story behind America's Obesity Epidemic.* New York: Oxford University Press, 2006.

Popkin, Barry. *The World Is Fat.* New York: Penguin, 2008.

Sassi, Franco. *Obesity and the Economics of Prevention: Fit Not Fat.* Paris: OECD, 2010.

Smil, Vaclav, and Kazuhiko Kobayashi. *Japan's Dietary Transition and Its Impacts.* Cambridge, MA: MIT Press, 2012.

The Politics of Farm Subsidies and Trade

Anderson, Kym. "Reducing Distortions to Agricultural Incentives: Progress, Pitfalls, Prospects." *American Journal of Agricultural Economics* 88, no. 5 (2006): 1135–1146.

Deere, Carolyn, and Daniel Esty, eds. *Greening the Americas.* Cambridge, MA: MIT Press, 2002.

Food First. *Food Sovereignty: A Right for All—Political Statement of the NGO/CSO Forum for Food Sovereignty.* Oakland, CA: Food First, June 14, 2002.

Gardner, Bruce L. *American Agriculture in the Twentieth Century: How It Flourished and What It Cost.* Cambridge, MA: Harvard University Press, 2002.

Honma, Masayoshi, and Yujiro Hayami. "The Determinants of Agricultural Protection Level: An Econometric Analysis." In *The Political Economy of Agricultural Protection,* edited by Kym Anderson and Yujiro Hayami. Sydney: Allen and Unwin, 1986.

Orden, David, Robert Paarlberg, and Terry Roe. *Policy Reform in American Agriculture: Analysis and Prognosis.* Chicago: University of Chicago Press, 1999.

Paarlberg, Robert. *Fixing Farm Trade: Policy Options for the United States.* New York: HarperCollins, 1987.

Tracy, Michael. *Government and Agriculture in Western Europe 1880–1988.* 3rd ed. New York: New York University Press, 1989.

Livestock, Meat, and Fish

Ausbel, Jesse H., Iddo K. Wernick, and Paul E. Waggoner. "Peak Farmland and the Prospect for Land Sparing." *Population and Development Review* 38, supplement, 2012. http://phe.rockefeller.edu/docs/PDR.SUPP%20Final%20Paper.pdf.

Burney, Jennifer, Steven Davis, and David Lobell. "Greenhouse Gas Mitigation by Agricultural Intensification." *PNAS*, 107, no. 26 (2010): 12052–12057.

Carson, Rachel. *Silent Spring*. Boston: Houghton Mifflin, 1962.

Cline, William. *Global Warming and Agriculture: Impact Estimates by Country*. Washington, DC: Peterson Institute, 2007.

Food and Agriculture Organization of the United Nations. *The State of the World's Land and Water Resources for Food and Agriculture*. Rome: FAO, 2011.

Masson, Jeffrey. *The Face on Your Plate: The Truth about Food*. New York: W. W. Norton, 2009.

Nelson, Gerald C., et al. *Climate Change: Impact on Agriculture and Costs of Adaptation*. Washington, DC: IFPRI, 2009.

Organisation for Economic Co-operation and Development. *Environmental Performance of Agriculture in OECD Countries since 1990*. Paris, 2008. www.oecd.org/tad/env/indicators.

Paarlberg, Robert. *Countrysides at Risk: The Political Geography of Sustainable Agriculture*. Baltimore, MD: Johns Hopkins University Press, 1996.

Pew Trusts. *Sustainable Marine Aquaculture*. Report of the Marine Aquaculture Task Force, Tacoma Park, MD, 2007.

Smaling, Eric, Moctar Toure, Nico de Ridder, Nteranya Sanginga, and Henk Breman. *Fertilizer Use and the Environment in Africa: Friends or Foes?* Background paper, African Fertilizer Summit. Abjua, Nigeria, June 9–13, 2006.

Steinfield, Henning, Pierre Gerber, Tom Wassenaar, Vincent Castel, and Mauricio Rosales. *Livestock's Long Shadow: Environmental Issues and*

Options. Rome: Food and Agriculture Organization of the United Nations, 2006.

Waldau, Paul. *Animal Rights: What Everyone Needs to Know*. New York: Oxford University Press, 2011.

Agribusiness, Supermarkets, and Fast Food

Belasco, Warren. *Appetite for Change: How the Counterculture Took on the Food Industry, 1966–1988*. New York: Pantheon, 1989.

Grey, Mark, A. "The Industrial Food Stream and Its Alternatives in the United States: An Introduction." *Human Organization* 59, no. 2 (Summer 2000): 143–150.

Reardon, Thomas, C. Peter Timmer, and Julio Berdegue. "The Rapid Rise of Supermarkets in Developing Countries." *Journal of Agricultural and Development Economics* 1, no. 2 (2004): 168–183.

Watson, James. *Golden Arches East: McDonald's in East Asia*. 2nd ed. Stanford, CA: Stanford University Press, 2006.

Organic and Local Food

Counihan, Carole. *Food Culture: A Reader*. 2nd ed. New York: Routledge, 2007.

Fromartz, Samuel. *Organic, Inc*. New York: Harcourt, 2006.

McWilliams, James E. *Just Food*. Boston: Little, Brown, 2009.

Pollan, Michael. *The Omnivore's Dilemma: A Natural History of Four Meals*. New York: Penguin, 2006.

Ronald, Pamela C., and Raoul W. Adamchak, *Tomorrow's Table: Organic Farming, Genetics, and the Future of Food*. New York: Oxford University Press, 2008.

Smil, Vaclav. "Global Population and the Nitrogen Cycle." *Scientific American* (July 1997): 76–81.

Smil, Vaclav. *Enriching the Earth, Fritz Haber, Carl Bosch, and the Transformation of World Food Production*. Cambridge, MA: MIT Press, 2001.

UNEP-UNCTAD. *Organic Agriculture and Food Security in Africa: Capacity-Building Task Force on Trade, Environment and Development*. New York and Geneva: United Nations, 2008.

USDA. "Local Food Systems: Concepts, Impacts, and Issues." ERS Report 97, May 2010.

Vogt, G. "The Origins of Organic Farming." In *Organic Farming: An International History*, edited by W. Lockeretz, 9–29. CABI, Oxfordshire, United Kingdom, 2008.

Williamson, Claire. "Is Organic Food Better for Our Health?" *Nutrition Bulletin* 32, no. 2 (2007): 104–108.

Winter, Carl K., and Sarah F. Davis. "Organic Foods." *Journal of Food Science* 7, no. 9 (2006): 117–124.

Food Safety and Genetically Engineered Food

Brookes, Graham, and Peter Barfoot. *GM Crops: The Global Socioeconomic and Environmental Impact—The First Nine Years 1996–2004*. Dorchester, UK: PG Economics, October 2005.

Huang, J., R. Hu, C. Fan, C. E. Pray, and S. Rozelle. "*Bt* Cotton Benefits, Costs, and Impacts in China," *AgBioForum* 5 no. 4 (2002): 153–166. http://www.agbioforum.org.

James, Clive. *Global Status of Commercialized Biotech/GM Crops*. ISAAA Brief 39. Ithaca, NY: International Service for the Acquisition of Agri-biotech Applications, 2008.

Jasanoff, Sheila. *Designs on Nature: Science and Democracy in Europe and the United States*. Princeton, NJ: Princeton University Press, 2005.

Mead, Paul S., Laurence Slutsker, Vance Dietz, Linda F. McCaig, Joseph S. Bresee, Craig Shapiro, Patricia M. Griffin, and Robert V. Tauxe. *Food-Related Illness and Death in the United States*. Atlanta, GA: Centers for Disease Control and Prevention, 2000. http://www.cdc.gov/ncidod/eid/v015n05/mead.htm.

Otsuki, Tsunehiro, John Wilson, and Mirvat Sewadeh. "Saving Two in a Billion: A Case Study to Quantify the Trade Effects of European Food Safety Standards on African Exports." Washington, DC: World Bank, DECRG, 2001.

Paarlberg, Robert. *The Politics of Precaution: Genetically Modified Crops in Developing Countries*. Washington, DC: International Food Policy Research Institute, 2001.

Paarlberg, Robert. *Starved for Science: How Biotechnology Is Being Kept Out of Africa*. Cambridge, MA: Harvard University Press, 2008.

Who Governs the World Food System?

Chicago Council on Global Affairs. *Renewing American Leadership in the Fight against Global Hunger and Poverty*. Chicago: Chicago Council on Global Affairs, 2009.

Easterly, William. *The White Man's Burden: Why the West's Efforts to Aid the Rest Have Done So Much Ill and So Little Good*. New York: Penguin, 2007.

Keck, Margaret E., and Kathryn Sikkink. *Activists beyond Borders: Advocacy Networks in International Politics*. Ithaca, NY: Cornell University Press, 1998.

Paarlberg, Robert. *Governance and Food Security in an Age of Globalization*. Food, Agriculture, and the Environment Discussion Paper 36. Washington, DC: International Food Policy Research Institute, 2002.

INDEX